MW00941683

Limitless

The Ultimate 5-Step System For Mastering The Law of
Attraction, Success and Manifesting Your Goals...Every Time!

(Part of The NLPQ Series: Volume 1)

Patrick Dahdal

ISBN:1495289559

ISBN-13:9781495289552

DISCLAIMER

DEDICATION

This book is dedicated to my wife, Marie Dahdal, who always believed in me from day one and stuck with me though my crazy ideas and ways of living. You make all the difference.

To my family who has always supported and been there for me. These are:

My mum (Anneli Bergquist) who shown me the power of thinking and being outside the box, and to go for what you believe in regardless of other people's opinions. Thank you for everything.

To LG and Adel Dahdal (my brother) as well as my family in the UK especially Maureen & David Blackwell. Thank you all for being there, none of this would have been possible without you.

I also want to dedicate this book to YOU. As a fellow brother and sister on this journey of awakening and exploring our potentials you are making a difference. My vision is that this difference you are making in your life will have a ripple effect onto your family, community and the world at large so we are creating a better future for all of us.

Lastly I want to dedicate this book to my father, George Dahdal, who unfortunately passed away at only 46 years old, but during his time here on earth has made big impact on my life by distilling in me that we are all unique, that I am unique and have a unique aspect to express. Thank you for being a great teacher even after your life on earth.

CONTENTS

ACKNOWLEDGMENTS

A big acknowledgement goes to all the great teachers I've been fortunate to be exposed to within the fields of psychology, applied psychology, NLP, Neuro-Semantics, biology, quantum physics, energy psychology, neuro-science and eastern philosophies. A special thank you goes to Stephen Wolinsky (the father of Quantum Psychology), Drs. Tad and Adriana James, Nisargadatta Maharaj, Dr. John Hagelin and Dr. Amit Goswami. To all my students who have attended my training and coaching programs. I've learnt from you all and this book wouldn't be possible without you. Thank you for enriching my life.

Chapter 1: Introduction

Welcome to the journey and adventure of YOU!

As you read through these pages and apply what's being shared your life will transform. The transformation will happen when you are living the five steps for mastering the law of attraction, success and manifesting your goals.

How do you live the five steps?

First, you must know them. This will happen automatically as you read the book. You will understand them and know them.

Secondly, you must apply them into your own life. Without any application of your understanding there's no transformation. You might get some mental 'highs' as you grasp a new cognition of what you read but there will be no stable transformation in your life. Transformation only happens when you are acting, behaving and walking through the world in a new way. This happens by applying what you are reading and learning here.

A great way to ensure you start to apply this into your life is keeping a journal. Journal your wins, aha-moments, new ideas and learning's. Ask yourself the question: 'How can I apply this to my life?' and journal your answer, then act on it. If the answer comes up in your mind 'I can't apply this', then ask yourself 'If I could apply into my own life, how would that play out?'. Keep asking and you'll get answer. Apply and transform.

What you must know before you read the book...

Before you continue reading this book it's important to get an overview of the five steps as well as how this book fits in to the context my overarching transformational system called NLPQ. This way you get an understanding of why it's laid out the way it is and this in turn will maximize the results you get from it.

Let's start with what NLPQ is?

NLPQ is a system that gives you the tools and knowledge to transform any area of your life or the life of anyone you choose to coach. It takes people from point A (their present reality) to point B (their desired reality) in the most effective and efficient manner possible by using the power of communication and change technology offered within the NLPQ system.

NLPQ is a system that takes into account all major components of the human system in its approach to change. The three major components are:

- The Mind System
- The Body System
- The Energy System

By using all three components NLPQ can create a faster, deeper and more importantly, a stable change in people's lives that will have an positive affect on their whole life situation not only the aspect they might have come to an NLPQ Practitioner for. It's in other words a holistic transformational system.

Let's have a quick look at each system...

The Mind System – this is how we use our internal pictures, sounds, feelings, perceptions, decisions, judgments, significances, evaluations, preferences to create our reality.

The Body System – this is how we use our physiology to create our reality and experience. The stronger and cleaner your physiology is the greater your experience of life is and how you use your physiology directly influences your experience of life moment by moment. A classic example is: you wake up in the morning and your experience before you have your first coffee is different than after you had it, right? The body system in action. Note: I'm not recommending coffee☺. There are better alternatives that doesn't harm your body system.

The Energy System – this is not something new but has been the most important aspect in Chinese medicine for thousands for years through practices such as acupuncture and Qi Gong. Here we look at the energy blockages both at a physiological level as well as a on a mental level. The basic principle here is that a negative experience (whether it's a limiting belief, negative emotion or thought that is triggered by a certain person, situation, place or event etc.) is a disruption in the energy system. This means that the cause of our 'negatives' is not the person, event or situation but the disruption of the energy system. By then handling the disruption by simple to use techniques we can have new empowered experiences in old situations that used to bring negative emotions and thoughts. Hope this makes sense, if not it will when we get to the energy aspect later in the book.

This was just a brief overview to give some context.

You could say that the mind and body system is the NLP part of NLPQ and that the energy system is the Q part of NLP. Even though there is an overlap due to that the human system is intertwined. An improvement of one system effects the other two systems and the reverse is true as well.

Let's dive into the...

The Ultimate 5-Step System For Mastering The Law of Attraction, Success and Manifesting Your Goals...Every Time!

Before I share with you the five steps, let me first say that these five steps are an application of NLPQ to the areas of success, goals and law of attraction. These steps can be applied to any area of your life with great results.

This book only presents a small fraction of the total body of knowledge that is NLPQ. However I wanted to share something that can dramatically improve your life hence I present to you the five steps.

DEFINE – The first step is define. Here we are defining the four most common and unconscious habits you are engaging in that is stopping your ability to master law of attraction, success and goals. We will also define the seven principles all masters are engaged in that will dramatically improve your ability. Once you know this you can stop the unconscious habits and start living the seven principles.

DETERMINE – The second step is to determine. Here I will share with you the quickest path to mastery, this goes beyond changing or fixing your beliefs, negative emotions or thoughts. These are only symptoms. In this section you'll discover what the one source of all your negatives are and determine the path you want to take to be free.

DELETE – The third step is to delete. Here I'll share with you an effective tool, validated by science, that will delete the negatives and limitations from your life. Once these are deleted you'll be in your full power to use the law of attraction, create the success you want and manifest the goals you desire. This is the section where the rubber meets the road.

DREAM – The fourth step is dreaming. Now you're ready to dream and decide what you want your life to be about. In this section we will design a life plan for you. By focusing on a life plan we are creating a balanced, harmonious and exciting vision for your life.

DECIDE – The fifth step is deciding. You've been letting go of your negatives, you are in your creative power and have tools to shape your future. Now the time has come to give yourself the gift of a deeper meaning for your life. The power of purpose. In this section you'll be discovering your life's purpose. This is an exciting segment you want to give yourself the time to go through in depth.

These are the five steps and we will go through them all in the following pages. However…

Here's what you need to know.

The book is divided into two sections. The first section is an introduction to NLP. If you're interested in how NLP can improve your personal, professional and business life then go ahead and read the book from 'Section 1' and onwards.

If you want to skip ahead to the five steps then go straight to 'Section 2'.

My recommendation is you read through the book from the beginning to the end and do all the exercises to the best of your ability. This way you're maximizing your experience and results.

Transform your life now!

Love to hear about your wins and gains. You can email to: wins@thelimitlessbook.com

To your abundance and freedom!

Patrick Dahdal

SECTION I

NLP

NLP=The Mind and Body Aspect of The Human System.

<u>This section covers</u>: A brief introduction to the standard NLP methodology.

Chapter 2: An Introduction To Neuro-Linguistic Programming (NLP)

Introduction

Today the world is fraught with people who are experiencing a variety of different problems. Many of these problems are holding people back from achieving their goals, their hopes and their dreams. In some cases, a variety of issues may be holding someone prisoner inside a network of unhealthy habits, negative thoughts, disempowering beliefs, common fears (e.g. fear of rejection, fear of success), addictions (e.g. smoking, over eating) and mental disorders including phobias.

There is absolutely no reason why anyone must put up with such problems any longer. NLP (Neuro Linguistic Programming) is an effective method that thousands of people around the world have turned to in the last few years in order to help them overcome a variety of different problems. While the techniques utilized in NLP are commonly used to treat problems such as fears and phobias, they are to a very high degree being used to assist with other problems and challenges; e.g. self-confidence, self-esteem, improved performance at work and in sports, communication and business. NLP has been used effectively help people to achieve success within business, career, leadership, sales, relationships, happiness and health to name a few. Many people have also turned to NLP in order to help them overcome bad habits, addictions and learning disabilities such as dyslexia.

NLP is also increasingly being used by many in the business world in order to help them develop a stronger rapport with clients and prospective clients and assist them in meeting their sales goals, increased creativity for business projects and strategy meetings. While NLP is certainly applicable in the business world, it can also be used personally in order to overcome barriers that may be holding you back and preventing you from enjoying a more fulfilling and satisfying life.

In the next several chapters we are going to explore the basis of NLP, what is involved in this method that so many top sports people, celebrities, politicians turn to for improved performance and how you can have it put to work in your own life in order to realize the goals and dreams you have.

Let's get started!

Part 1

What is NLP?

Neuro-linguistic programming, often referred to simply as NLP, is a methodology for creating your desired results. It looks at the way in which the mind works in order to create specific results. For example; in NLP we look at how and study how someone overcame a phobia (as opposed to study people who currently have a phobia) because once we can find out how they achieved that specific result of overcoming a phobia we can deconstruct the process and replicate it in other people who have a phobia now and cure it under 60 minutes. This is what makes NLP so effective is that it allows us to create rapid change due to knowing the exact formula someone has to produce a specific result and then by using the NLP methodology of modeling we can replicate that formula on anyone else.

The founders of NLP are John Grinder and Richard Bandler. It was through the study of what the most successful people in the world did in order to produce a desired results that neruo-linguistic programming was born. Grinder and Bandler studied the behavior as well as the patterns and language of successful people and were able to deconstruct that behavior in order to model and then reproduce each strategy.

How is NLP Used?

Today, NLP is used to address a variety of different issues (negative emotions and beliefs that is holding one back) and is also the place to go to when you want to improve any and all aspects of life. In addition, NLP is also used effectively for deeper issues such disabilitating fears and anxieties, limiting decisions we made in the past that is still controlling our thoughts and behaviors, and preventing us for operating at our peaks.

NLP can also be used to communicate in a more effective manner, improve motivation and improve problem solving skills. Other benefits of NLP can include developing leadership skills, relieving stress and meeting one's goals.

Ultimately, NLP involves studying the way in which we interpret and then relate to the world around us and how we can change that process to create the emotions, behaviors and habits that is aligned with the results we want to have created. It should be fully understood that NLP is not an abstract form of simply theoretical knowledge. By understanding the models involved in NLP, it is possible to gain control over the way in which the human brain makes sense of an experience and then taking action in order to change that experience.

NLP can be utilized in a variety of different settings and in many different environments. It is commonly used in business, personal development, coaching, communication, increased performance at the workplace, leadership and management, sales, sports, creating wealth and personal growth. As the benefits of NLP has come to be more widely known it has now entered the educational system as an effective way of teaching both in schools and universities worldwide as an example NLP can be used to handle dyslexia, anxiety for learning or performing at tests etc., this is why it has become so popular.

The Foundations of NLP

Communication Models

There are two different models of communication that are utilized in NLP. The first model is known as the Meta Model and involves a process of developing and then refining precision in communication through language as well as meaning. It's a way of asking questions and listening that gives us as NLP Practitioners the ability to cut through the 'fluff' in a communication and quickly get to the core of the matter. The Meta Model also gives us the map we can use when listening to someone speaking and get a good understanding of their model of the world and the keys to why they might be experiencing the problems or challenges they share with us. By us then asking the right questions we can dismantle what is holding them back in a certain situation e.g. performing in sales etc. It is of course much more to the Meta Model. We will be covering more on the Meta Model later.

The other model used in NLP is the Milton Model which involves abstract and vague language that is artfully communicated. In this model supplied meaning is deliberately lacking, allowing the listener to provide their own meaning instead of relying upon supplied meaning. This communication model is commonly used for hypnosis, communication and influence, and assisting clients to create deeper change and transformation.

If you're interested more about the communication models I have a gift for you. You'll get free access to my mini-communication course called 'The Secrets of Magical Communication' where you can learn more about NLP and communication. Go to this link to watch the videos:

http://www.TheLimitlessProgram.com/bookbonuses

Presuppositions Of NLP

Presuppositions are also an important element in understanding NLP. Presuppositions, in terms of NLP, are sets of beliefs which are modeled upon the working beliefs of the top two therapists which were initially studied in the creation of NLP. It is important to understand that these are beliefs only, not truths. This is crucial to the foundation of NLP. There are no truths in NLP, there is only what works and doesn't work. In NLP we use what works and what produces excellent results. This is what is shared in NLP; Models of Excellence as it relates to all facets and areas of life.

The NLP Presuppositions are conveniently held assumptions that when being assumed by us practitioners or coaches in NLP, produces amazing results for our clients.

Here are the foundational NLP presuppositions as an introduction to the topic (to understand the real power of the NLP presuppositions is to go to an NLP Practitioner Training, where you'll have an experience of them):

1.   Respect for the other person's model of the world.

2.   Behavior and change are to be evaluated in terms of context, and Ecology

3.   Resistance in a client is a Sign of a lack of rapport. (There are no resistant clients, only inflexible communicators. Effective communicators accept and utilize all communication presented to them.)

4.   People are not their behaviors. (Accept the person; change the behavior.)

5.   Everyone is doing the best they can with the resources they have available. (Behavior is geared for adaptation, and present behavior is the best choice available. Every behavior is motivated by a positive intent.)

6.   Calibrate on Behavior: The most important information about a person is that person's behavior.

7.   The map is not the Territory. (The words we use are NOT the event or the item they represent.)

8. (U) You are in charge of your mind, and therefore your results (and I am also in charge of my mind and therefore my results).

9. People have all the Resources they need to succeed and to achieve their desired outcomes. (There are no unresourceful people, only unresourceful states.)

10. All procedures should increase Wholeness

11. There is ONLY feedback! (There is no failure, only feedback.)

12. The meaning of communication is the Response you get.

13. The Law of Requisite Variety! (The system/person with the most flexibility of behavior will control the system.)

14. All procedures should be Designed to increase choice.

Submodalities

It is also important to understand the way in which we present as well as re-present our experiences to both our conscious as well as our unconscious mind via our senses. While it is widely accepted that we make sense of the world around us through our senses, in NLP we discovered that how we re-present the information coming through our senses directly determine our experience, behavior and thought patterns. In NLP we call this submodalities.

Submodalitties form the building blocks of all of our sensory experiences. Imagine a car in your mind. Consider the many ways in which you can change the representation of the car (e.g. you can make it blue or red, big or small) in your mind without actually changing the content (the car) of that representation?

To further clarify this...

You could make the car a lighter or darker color. You could also make the car either smaller or bigger. You might also change the location of the car in your mind's eye, that is you could make it seem further away or really close up. By making all of these changes, you are able to change the meaning of the representation of the car.

While a car is an object that is somewhat neutral, it does represent a good example of the ways in which sensory submodalities exist within the use of language as well as the way in which we understand metaphors.

Uniqueness

It is also crucial to understand that the submodalities used by every individual are completely unique. In addition, they are also continually evolving and changing. As a result, it is not possible to generalize in an accurate manner. It is possible; however, to carefully utilize the Meta Model in order to establish the precise way in which each person actually constructs their own model of reality.

Once you understand the way in which someone makes sense of their own personal world, you will be able to communicate with that person on a level that is more meaningful. This technique can be extremely helpful in the sales world in order to understand the way clients think and improve sales.

Submodalities allows us to create rapid change for ourselves and our clients. We can change disempowering habits (e.g. nail biting, unwanted emotions in specific situations) and beliefs within minutes.

Because with submodalities we are not working on the content of a problem (like in traditional psychology) instead we are working on the actual structure of the problem. This is work on structure instead of content is what makes NLP such an effective model that produces fast results.

What we covered so far are some of the basic building blocks of NLP. When used together they form a powerful tool that can help anyone to achieve greater success.

Who can Benefit from NLP?

As we have previously discussed, the numbers of people who are benefiting from NLP are rapidly increasing as more and more people begin to understand that NLP can be applied to a wide range of life situations. Just some of the individuals who may be able to benefit from NLP include:

• Anyone who interacts with other people

• Anyone who has a desire to improve their ability to interact and connect with others

• Anyone who is searching for a way to achieve personal growth

• Anyone who wishes for their past to no longer prevent them from achieving their goals

• Anyone who wishes to be the best they can be

• Anyone who wants to get more out of life

As you can see, these are a diverse range of situations in which individuals can benefit from NLP. The people who commonly benefit from NLP actually do come from a variety of different backgrounds as well as interests, such as:

• **Parents** - Parents who take advantage NLP in their parenting are often able to feel more at ease and comfortable in modeling the behaviors that they would like for their children to emulate. In addition, they are also likely to feel more comfortable in knowing how to influence their children in a positive way to give the values and habits that will assist them in their life and school. Parents also use NLP to teach their children practical skills that will assist their children with problems in school, learning difficulties and social problems.

• **Personal Growth & Personal Development** – anyone wanting to improve their life or areas of their life will greatly benefit from the tools NLP offer. By using all the tools, models and strategies of NLP a person will experience a dramatic change in their life. This is why NLP has been so popular in the personal growth field and the number one source for top coaches worldwide.

• **Trainers and Educators** - anyone in the training or educational field who wants to learn more about the strategies that actually help people to learn in a more effective fashion will benefit from the use of NLP.

• **Students** - regardless of where you are in your education, if you are interested in learning how to integrate new methods for effectively coping with the pressures of the learning environment as well as learning how to take advantage of the learning process in a more direct fashion, NLP is for you.

• **Mental Health Professionals/Coaches** - mental health professionals and coaches can utilize NLP in order to learn how to provide themselves with improved care while also providing their clients with new and improved skills and insights. They can also use the many NLP models for creating rapid and lasting changes for their clients.

• **Medical practitioners** - through the use of NLP, medical practitioners can learn how they can establish improved rapport with their patients while also gaining a greater understanding of the role that beliefs can actually play in the patient's health and recovery-

• **Business people and Managers** - NLP can be used to enhance communication and presentation skills while also building teams that are more resourceful and strong as well as improve performance of staff.

• **Salespeople** - individuals involved in sales will gain the ability to establish deep rapport with clients and prospects in a more effective fashion by determining the expectations and the needs of the clients using for example the Meta Model. They will also learn how to position their service or product in order to meet the needs of the clients as well by using unconscious language and the Milton Model.

• **Entertainers and Athletes** - anyone involved in athletics or the entertainment field can benefit from NLP by learning how to improve their focus on their desired goals, making use of their inner resources and identifying the strategies that will support the goals. NLP can also assist in accelerating the process of achieving ones goals.

Part 2

The Meta Model

What is the Meta Model?

The Meta Model is one of several models that is utilized in NLP. It involves a set of precise process for questioning as well as listening. The Meta Model set of questions will change how the client or the person communicating to perceives their world e.g. their problems or limitations will disappear or at the minimum not have the hold it might have had in the past.

Sometimes just using the Meta Model itself can be the solution and if the presented problem or challenge isn't solved the Meta Model has loosened up the clients model of the world so other NLP tools can be used with high degree of effectiveness to blow the clients problem, challenge, obstacle or limitation.

The Goal of the Meta Model

The goal of the Meta Model is to understand the perspective of the individual. When an individual describes issues or problems which he faces, that person will typically constrain the words that are used to describe the experience. In most cases, the individual will describe the situation in a manner that is closely related to his or her own understanding of that experience. They will not typically provide all of the details that occurred during that particular experience.

In this type of situation, someone who was trained in NLP would work to retrieve the information that was not revealed by coming to an increased understanding of the language patterns used by the individual. A set of questions would also be asked to retrieve the information that was not initially provided.

In addition, the person using NLP would also take care to listen to the word choices used by the client in response to those questions. This method helps the individual to eventually retrieve their own underlying thoughts and understand more about their perception of the issue so that they can then convert those perceptions into words, which will allow them to resolve the problem.

The ultimate goal of NLP through the use of the Meta Model is to bring out beliefs that may be restrictive as well as fears that may be deeply rooted within or other mental limitations presented by the client. It is critical to understand that the words that are selected by the individual can be very valuable in terms of indicating that person's perception of the world. Listening is often the cornerstone of this model because it allows a practitioner of NLP to understand more about the individual's model of the world by carefully listening to the words that are selected.

The practitioner must ensure that they do not bring their own point of view, perception or beliefs into the situation. Bringing one's own set of beliefs into the situation will make it difficult to recover the information from the client that could prove to be critical to retrieving that crucial information.

Part 3

An Introduction To Basic NLP Techniques

A variety of different techniques can be used in the practice of NLP. The goal of these techniques is to understand the psyche of the person in order to modify patterns of behavior and thought so that the goals of the client can be accomplished and so that positive changes can be brought about within that person's life.

It is often stated in NLP that the perception of one's experience depends on the interpretation of external stimuli through our senses and filters (example of filters are our beliefs, values, emotional state etc). As a result, one's response to an experience is entirely dependent upon our perceived image of the world around us, utilizing feelings, emotions, thoughts, etc.

When an experience is put into words, the words become the critical indicators of the feelings and thoughts that were experienced during a particular event. As a result, listening and then questioning and later understanding the language that is used by an individual makes it possible to establish a model of that person's behavior and their response to an event.

It is then possible to analyze that model and consequently eliminate problems that may be experienced by the individual. It is also possible to model positive areas of behavior and then reproduce that same model and apply it toward negative areas within one's life in order to bring about change or improvement.

It has been noted that someone who is successful may exhibit particular beliefs or behavior or even thoughts. The basis of NLP relies upon the idea that if we are able to model those attributes that are inherent to success then we will then be able to apply them to our lives on a daily basis. This makes it possible for each one of us to achieve the peak of success we desire.

The Map

One of the most important aspects of NLP is the idea of a map. The map is our personal perception of the world (including self, others, environment, what capabilities we have or don't have, what abilities we have or don't have etc). Our map is the perception of the world not the actuality of the world. The map concept is also part of the NLP Presuppositions we talked about earlier: The map is not the territory.

This concept of the map was first derived from Alfred Korzybski's work in General Semantics. Basically it states that the way we organize our map (our maps where created unconsciously and then taken on as the truth) is how we will interact with the world. For example if a person's map says: 'All politicians are evil' then when that person interacts with a politician their map will determine the feeling and behaviors this person exhibits in that interaction. Another person might have a map that says: 'I'm too young to be a life coach' then this person's behavior and feelings will effect what actions and how those actions are carried out when it comes to being a life coach. It will limit their success and performance.

Our maps are filters e.g. beliefs, emotional states in specific situations, values, language and more; due to this our map is either empowering or disempowering us depending on the results we want to create. This could potentially be the root of an individual's problems which are holding him or her back from achieving their goals and attaining success.

The map of someone who is successful will contain an appropriate set of values, thoughts and feelings. That same map could potentially be translated to a completely different person in order to bring about the same types of results. It is entirely possible to change the map of a person, or their own portrait of how they view the world, in order to elicit a certain positive attitude or behavior.

A variety of techniques can be utilized in order to create a change in the person's map and NLP has all the tools to create this change easily and effectively. This means that you can change your map so it is aligned with your life goals and in alignment with the success you want to create. The map you carry around will determine the life you'll experience.

Anchoring

Anchoring is one of the techniques that is commonly used in NLP. This technique depends upon the way in which an individual will commonly establish an anchor or form an association between their emotional state of mind and a sound, sight, touch or smell (an external stimulus). Once that association has been formed, each time that the person experiences that specific external stimulus he or she will immediately make a connection to the specified anchor (which again can be a sound, sight, touch or smell). Consider, for example, the way in which a particular smell or song can bring you right back to a particular time in the past. This is an example of anchoring that many people commonly experience.

As a result of anchoring, the stimulus can come to be viewed as a trigger for a particular emotional state or feeling. Through the use of this technique, an NLP Practitioner would then be able to create an anchor deliberately within the client in order to trigger a specific stimulus in order to help the patient achieved a desired state of mind or emotion.

For example: A client comes to you with the problem of being nervous when talking to their manager about a pay rise. You as an NLP Practitioner can then use the anchoring process to create powerful states of confidence and certainty, and then associate these states to the event when the client is talking to the manager so that the states of confidence and certainty is present and the old state of being nervous is gone. This will then allow the client to be in their highest performance when negotiating their pay rise.

This is just one example of how you can use anchoring. The anchoring process can be applied to many of changes your client wants achieve. It plays a central role in NLP.

The Swish Pattern

The Swish Pattern is another technique that is also commonly used in NLP. This technique utilizes a train of thought that can be modified so that a behavior or emotional state that is considered to be undesirable can then be converted into a behavior or emotional state that is desirable. Many times a visual cue will be used with this technique and is commonly used to eradicate unwanted habits such as addiction, drinking, smoking, over-eating, etc.

Through the use of the swish pattern, the brain is programmed to actually change from a pattern of thought that is negative or a negative image over to a positive image or train of thought. In addition to visual cues, auditory sounds may also be used in order to enhance the efficacy of the method.

For example, a person would think of something that they would like to improve and then they would picture themselves as having that positive result they desired. Each time the person encounters the negative old image, the mind will automatically and immediately (after doing the swish pattern) change over to the positive image (the results the client desires). This will help the person to eliminate their problems, whether they be worries, addictions or fears.

Reframing

Reframing is another effective technique we use in NLP. This technique works to change the perception of an individual regarding an event, which can then change the underlying meaning of the event. In most cases, in changing the meaning of the event it will be possible to change the person's response in terms of feelings and emotions. As a result, behavior may also be changed as well.

Through the use of the reframing technique, the person has an opportunity to view the world through an entirely new perspective. This can actually provide that person with new meaning within their own life. Common examples of the way in which reframing is used includes mythological stories, children's stories, fairy tales, etc.

There is actually a six-step reframing process which is based on the precept that even though behaviors can be undesirable, the intention of the person exhibiting the behaviors is typically positive. NLP strives to identify the intention behind the behavior by using a reframing process.

A practitioner trained in NLP can determine the behaviors that are positive and help the individual to fulfill the same intention by simply substituting more positive behaviors.

The Well Formed Outcome

The purpose of this NLP process is to assist our clients in accelerating their goals achievement and also to ensure they really considered all consequences of achieving that goal. For example you might get a client who says their goal is to have more energy all the time. However if they had energy all the time this might affect their sleep. Which in turns will make them more tired in the long run. From a well formed outcome perspective we would maybe change the goal to 'have more energy when I need it and a relaxed state when going to sleep'. This is a simple example just to give you an idea of how this process works.

When using the well-formed outcome process the client will be asked to view the desired outcome and then analyze the effect of that outcome on the world (self, family, others, environment etc.). They are then asked to determine how feasible it would be to achieve that outcome. It is crucial that the outcome that is identified by the client to be completely achievable and also within the capacity of that individual.

In addition, the outcome must also include effects that are positive and can be controlled in all stages by the client. This is important in order to achieve the goal. Many goals don't come to fruition due to this fact alone.

Parts Integration

Parts integration is one of the most popular techniques in NLP as it produces deep changes within the person and in such a short time. This technique is based on the idea that our different personal characteristics will always be in disagreement. The assumption of this technique is that our internal conflicts comes about as a direct result of our diverse perceptions and attitudes of the external world. An example of this could be:

"I really want to start this business but a part of me feels like I won't be successful"

Here you got an internal conflict. On one hand the client wants to start their business on the other hand the client feels like he or she won't be successful. This leads to not starting at all, procrastinating, getting distracted or starting but not following through.

The goal of parts integration is to attempt to integrate those different parts of the client. The part that wants to start the business and the part that believes it won't be successful.

What the parts integration does is taking the different aspects of our individual personalities that are incongruent in order to create a congruent whole. This is accomplished by identifying the different elements and then converting those elements into a single harmonious state. At this point the internal conflict will be resolved. As a result a state of mental peace will be achieved.

The Metaphor

The metaphor is another very effective process used in NLP. This process primarily makes use of anecdotes and metaphors in order to make a connection within the unconscious mind. Through the use of metaphors, an NLP Practitioner would be able to (after the practitioner has identified the beliefs that are inherent to an individual along with the values, thoughts and assumptions that are underlying a particular behavior that is undesirable) to create change in the clients unconscious mind even though the clients conscious minds hears a story or anecdote. This is a very powerful way of creating change within the client as it works directly with the unconscious mind where all changes takes place.

Summary

As you can see, there is a variety of different tools that are commonly used in order to make the best use NLP and we have only covered a fraction of what's available.

The precise type of technique that is used depends upon the individual, the problems they face and the desired outcomes that are sought.

In the next section, we will delve more deeply into the different aspects of NLP.

Part 4

NLP Communication & Persuasion

It has often been said that persuasion is an art. When it comes to NLP that is certainly the case. Like most art forms, persuasion is typically only mastered by a few individuals. In many cases, most people engage in communication that is lacking in skill and tact.

As the modern world moves forward and becomes more complex, it has become increasingly important for individuals to learn how to function in a fashion that allows for communication that is more witty, tactful and skillful. It is also crucial to learn how to persuade as well as influence, especially in the world of business and the workplace.

Today more than ever we are bombarded with messages and not all messages we receive are for our own best interest. This is another reason to understand the NLP communication and persuasion skills as you then can identify when someone is trying to influence or persuade you and decide yourself if you want to receive that message or not.

If there were only two skills you would want to master that would have the biggest impact on your life those would be:

1)   Mastery of communication and persuasion

2)   Mastery of your emotional states

Because if you can have the feelings you want whenever you want at your disposal and the ability to communicate effectively and get your message across and accepted (e.g. when you're negotiating a pay rise, influencing your kids to make a better decision or making a business deal) then there is nothing you can't achieve.

Mastery of communication and persuasion is essential if you want to have the edge in today's society. In this section, we are going to take a closer look at precisely why these skills are so helpful and how NLP can help you to master the art of persuasion.

The Basics of Persuasion

As we saw in the previous section, NLP makes use of a variety of effective techniques. All of these techniques utilize a number of specific patterns present within language, including reframing, metaphor and anchoring. NLP persuasion techniques can be utilized in business for a variety of purposes. Some of these purposes include improving sales and convincing others to consider your position.

In addition, the persuasion techniques that are used in NLP can also be used on a more personal level in order to heal an individual who is suffering from low self-esteem or confidence, disempowering beliefs or phobias. You can use these persuasion techniques in order to help a client to achieve a more positive attitude and behavior.

Do you ever feel as though you could have chosen better words when speaking with someone? If so, you are certainly not alone. Many of us feel that way from time to time. The reason is that our communication methods are often lacking and do not contain a solid plan. We might use statement that is generalized rather than specific. The result of generalized statements is that it is impossible for them to be true but they cause havoc in our communication. A common example would be a statement that begins with "You always...."

While it may be true that someone sometimes exhibits a particular behavior, it is not true that they ALWAYS exhibit that behavior. The use of such a statement reveals a lack of sensitivity as well as sensibility and yet it is a common occurrence within our modes of communication. This is an ineffective form of communication that can leave a bad impression.

It is crucial to understand that all humans have the ability to influence other humans. In fact, it is impossible an individual to not have an influence on another person. The influence in question could be negative or positive, but it is there nonetheless. The influence could also be varied.

It our language, words, emotional states, physiology and intention that makes our communication with another either a negative or a positive experience. It should be kept in mind that even during times when we are not communicating through the use of language, we are still communicating. This is accomplished through the use of body language. Although less specific than verbal communication, body language can still possess the power to make a difference regarding the way another person feels as well as the way that they perceive you.

The Intent Behind NLP Persuasion

The intent behind the NLP persuasion model is to create positive change and results whether in business or personal change work. The persuasion skill is a powerful tool and should be treated as such. That is only use it for good.

In this section we are not going to focus on all aspects of The NLP Communication and Persuasion model as that can cover volumes of books on its own and this is just an introduction.

Instead I'm going share with you the foundations of communication you must have in place for any successful communication and persuasion, rapport.

The Foundation Is Rapport

First step to be able to create rapport is to understand what we in NLP call our representational systems. Each of use our senses to make sense of the world. Those are see, hear, feel, touch and smell. We then re-present (represent) the information from the external world to ourselves via our senses. These are our representational systems.

When we communicate and use language (words) we tend to have a preferred way of using words and our body, which we call modes of operation. The three major modes of operating and communicating are:

Visual (see)

Auditory (hear)

Kinesthetic (feel)

Let's go through, the three major modes of operation so you can notice what mode people are operating in, and begin to identify them. You can then begin to match the modes by using the predicates (seeing, hearing or feeling words) and physiology (body posture and movements) that match their representational system.

Visual

Typically, people who are in a visual mode stand, or sit, with their heads and/or bodies erect with their eyes up, and will be breathing from the top of their lungs. They often sit forward in the chair or on the edge of the chair. They tend to be more organized, neat, well-groomed and orderly. More deliberate. More appearance oriented, and sometimes quieter. Good spellers. Memorize by seeing pictures, and are less distracted by noise. Often have trouble remembering verbal instructions, and are bored by long verbal explanations because their minds tend to wander. They would rather read than be read to. A visual person will be interested in how someone looks at them, and will respond to being taken places, and being bought things. They will tend to use words like: see 'ya later, I want to look at it, focus on it, watch it, be clear, foggy, picture that, notice, appears.

Auditory

Someone who is auditory will move their eyes sideways and also down to the right. They breathe from the middle of the chest. They typically talk to themselves, and are easily distracted by noise. They often move their lips when they say words. They can repeat things back to you easily. They may find math and writing more difficult and spoken language easier. They like music and learn by listening. They memorize by steps, procedures, and sequence. An auditory person is often interested in being told how they're doing, and responds to a certain set of words or tone of voice. They tend to use words and phrases like: listen, talk to, said, speak, hear, and sounds like, "Good to talk to you."

Kinesthetic

They will typically be breathing from the bottom of their lungs, so you'll see their stomach go in and out as they breathe. Their posture is often more slumped over, and they often move and talk verrrry slooowly. They will typically access their feelings and emotions to "get a feel" for what they're doing. They respond to physical rewards, and touching. They also stand close to people and touch them. They are often physically oriented people (athletes). They may move a lot, and they memorize by doing, or walking through something. They use words like: feelings, get in touch, hold, grasp, and handle.

Those are the characteristics of the three major modes of operation. And so, the question is now, how do you use them to communicate with people? How do you communicate with someone who is primarily in one of those modes? This brings us to the subject of rapport.

Think of it! If there's anything that you want to get, or if there's anything you need, then you will probably need someone's help in getting it. This is true whether you're a salesperson, a teacher or even a carpenter. No matter what you do, the ability to develop and maintain rapport with the large numbers of people of varying backgrounds will allow you to get what you want. Having rapport with someone will allow you to do anything. So, rapport is probably the most important skill on the planet.

The basis of rapport is that when people are like each other, they like each other. When people are not like each other, they don't like each other. When you like someone, you are willing to assist them in having whatever they want. Remember that 38% of all communication is tone of voice, and 55% is physiology. So, most communication is outside of our conscious awareness. A tremendous opportunity exists for communication outside of normal channels, and that's what rapport is all about.

For the sake of contrast please remember a time when you were accessing your feelings, in a feeling state, of calm and quiet. Was there a time when you were in this state, and perhaps you can recall being with another person who was in an excited (visual) mode. Do you remember the feelings in your body when that happened?

Or can you remember being in a really excited (Visual) mode, and talking to someone in a real slow (Kinesthetic) state. Remember how it drove you crazy waiting for the other person to catch up?

Please, remember that neither of these modes of operation is wrong, they're just how people operate. To be a master communicator, you will also need to keep in mind that you will communicate best with people, when you employ their primary modality.

Too often, however, communication takes place in a system where people are unconsciously mis-matching modalities. So the first major element of rapport is to match the modality the person is in.

If you're meeting with someone, for example, who is in high visual, and you're not quite there, sit up in your chair, breathe from the top of your lungs, and be excited. Or at least act in a way that matches what they're doing. On the other hand, if you're meeting with someone who is auditory, you want to slow down a bit, modulate your voice more, and "listen, really listen." If you're meeting with someone who is kinesthetic, slow waaay dooown. And talk to them about feelings. Actually change your voice tone so that it matches theirs, and really "get a sense of it."

On the next two pages are lists of predicates, and predicate phrases. Look at these now, and notice the words and phrases that people use in each major representational system. In each major representational system, people are using different words, different phrases that actually reveal what's going on inside their heads.

List of Predicates

VISUAL AUDITORY KINESTHETIC UNSPECIFIED

VISUAL	AUDITORY	KINESTHETIC	UNSPECIFIED
see	hear	feel	sense
look	listen	touch	experience
view	sound(s)	grasp	understand
appear	make music	get hold of	think
show	harmonize	slip through	learn
dawn	tune in/out	catch on	process
reveal	be all ears	tap into	decide
envision	rings a bell	make contact	motivate
illuminate	silence	throw out	consider
imagine	be heard	turn around	change
clear	resonate	hard	perceive
foggy	deaf	unfeeling	insensitive
focused	mellifluous	concrete	distinct
hazy	dissonance	scrape	conceive
crystal	question	get a handle	know
picture	unhearing	solid	

List of Predicate PHRASES

VISUAL	AUDITORY	KINESTHETIC
An eyeful	Afterthought	All washed up
Appears to me	Blabbermouth	Boils down to
Bird's eye view	Clearly expressed	Come to grips with
Catch a glimpse of	Call on	Control yourself
Clear cut	Describe in detail	Cool/calm/collected
Dim view	Earful	Firm foundations
Flashed on	Give an account of	Get a handle on
Get a perspective on	Give me your ear	Get a load of this
Get a scope on	Grant an audience	Get in touch with
Hazy Idea	Heard voices	Get the drift of
Horse of a different color	Hidden message	Get your goat
In light of	Hold your tongue	Hand in hand
In person	Idle talk	Hang in there
In view of	Inquire into	Heated argument
Looks like	Keynote speaker	Hold it!
Make a scene	Loud and clear	Hold on!
Mental image	Manner of speaking	Hothead
Mental picture	Pay attention to	Keep your shirt on
Mind's eye	Power of speech	Know-how
Naked eye	Purrs like a kitten	Lay cards on table
Paint a picture	State your purpose	Pain-in the neck
See to it	Tattle-tale	Pull some strings
Short sighted	To tell the truth	Sharp as a tack

The second element of rapport is physical mirroring of the individual's physiology. Actually physically copying their posture, facial expressions, hand gestures and movements, and their eye blinking will cause their body to say unconsciously to their mind, "Hey, (s)he's like me!" It's undeniable to the nervous system.

The third element is to match their voice: The tone, tempo, timbre (quality of the voice), and the volume. You can also match their key words. Perhaps they often say, "Actually." You can use it in a sentence several times. Say it back to them.

The fourth element is to match their breathing. You can actually pace someone's breathing by breathing at exactly the same time as they do (matching the in and out breath). By matching their breathing, by pacing their breathing, you can then begin to lead them out of the representational system they're in, into another one.

The fifth element is to match the size of the pieces of information (chunk size or level of abstraction) they deal with. If someone usually deals in the big picture, they will probably be bored with the details. On the other hand someone who is into details will find that there's not enough information to deal with, if you only give them the big picture. So make sure that you are matching the content chunks that the person deals with.

The sixth element is to match their common experiences. This is what's usually called rapport. When people first meet, often their early relationship is about matching common experiences, common interests, background, and beliefs and values and their ideologies and common associations.

Those are the critical elements of rapport. Next, how do I establish rapport, and then how do I know when I'm in rapport (see next segment about Sensory Acuity)?

To establish rapport, the process is to match and mirror completely, what the other person is doing. When I'm training people in rapport skills they often ask, "Well how can I do that, they'll think I'm making fun of them." You do need to be subtle when doing matching and mirroring, but typically most people are in a trance when talking anyway. They're so caught up in what they're going to say next that they are rarely fully aware of what you're doing. And if they do, you can have a good laugh about it.

Part 6

Sensory Acuity through NLP

In terms of NLP, sensory acuity refers to the ability to examine, observe and then interpret cues that are delivered externally. This skill is used in NLP in order to train one's mind to see as well as listen to forms of communication that are non-verbal, such as eye movements, body language, etc.

Although they are often unaware of it, everyone exhibits cues externally. Such unconscious cues can reflect the state of the internal mind as well as the thought process of that individual. As one increases their sensory acuity, it becomes possible to read those cues in a more efficient manner.

A wide variety of different cues can be emitted through nonverbal forms of communication. As a result, it is imperative that one learns to master sensory acuity in order to become the most proficient communicator possible. When we make an effort to hone our sensory acuity skills, it becomes possible to interpret the signals that we receive in a very effective fashion and then utilize that information in order to form more effective responses and communication.

It is only possible to form a complete image of communication when verbal cues as well as non-verbal signals are taken into consideration. A host of information can be learned from an individual simply by considering what they are actually saying, how they are saying it along with what they are not saying. By understanding and then implementing all of the forms of communication, it becomes possible to become a master communicator as well as to develop stronger and deeper relationships with people.

The Steps Involved in Developing Sensory Acuity

In order to become proficient at sensory acuity, it is important to make sure that you are dedicated to practicing the skill. This is not a skill that can be mastered overnight. You will need to invest some time in it and in a good NLP Practitioner training you'll be mastering this skill.

Ideally, it is best if you start out small. Instead of trying to focus on all of the elements of communication, it is typically a good idea to focus on only a few areas to observe and then over time begin to build upon that so that you are able to master the whole skill.

One problem that many people frequently face when using this technique is that they are not sure whether they should focus their attention upon the person or on what the person is saying. There is often a concern that if you focus too much on what the person is saying you could miss an important nonverbal cue and vice versa. This skill requires practice as you must develop the ability to listen to the structure of the language and at the same time listen to the content of what's being said as well as all the non-verbal cues. With practice you'll get to the stage where all of this is happening simultaneously and effortlessly. This is when you start to really master the art of communication.

The Five Fundamental Areas of Observation

There are five critical areas of observation (and in NLP we call the observation skill calibration) that should be incorporated when communication with others. You want to pay attention to their:

• Breathing
• Color changes

- Muscle changes

- Facial Tone changes

- Changes in Lower Lip Area

Breathing

The breathing pattern of the speaker can provide you with many clues. Those patterns can tell you a lot about that person's state of mind. When you notice that there has been some type of variation in the other person's breathing, it is imperative to take note of where the person's breathing is derived from. For example, are they breathing from their chest or their stomach? There may also be a change in their rate of breathing as well. Consider where in the conversation you first noticed the change in breathing. This can help you to understand what it was about the conversation that caused an internal change in their state of mind.

By paying careful attention to the breathing rate of an individual, you will have a good idea of what they are thinking before they tell you verbally.

Not sure you will be able to notice if a person's breathing has change? Try to keep an eye on the rise and fall of their shoulders. This is an easy way to see breathing changes as well as a change in their mental state.

Color Changes

Although you may not have ever noticed, everyone is comprised of different tones and shades of colors. Skin tone is never a single shade. In order to more accurately assess a person's mental state, it is important to take note of how the colors of the skin tone on the face may change from one moment to another. In most cases, a person will experience different skin tones based on their emotions. Once you begin to pay attention to these changes, you will be in a better position to take note of any changes before they are verbally expressed.

Muscle Changes

The muscles that are present within the face can also provide you with a great deal of information. Although the muscles within the face are typically quite small, minute really, they can still be quite helpful. Keep an eye on the muscles that are located near the jaw line as well as on the outer corners of the eyes and around the mouth. These muscles will immediately reveal to you when someone has become tense. In addition, you may notice that the muscles in the forehead begin to crease as tension increases. As you practice observing these minute muscle areas, you will become much more adept at identifying changes in emotions based on the topic of conversation.

Changes in the Lower Lips

The lower lips can also provide you with a great deal of information. The reason for this is that it is actually quite difficult to consciously control the lower lip. When you notice the shape as well as the size, color and movement of the lower lip, you will be able to interpret the emotions of the other person.

Vocal Tones

Of course, most of us are already aware that the sound of one's voice can be a big tip off regarding changes in emotions. As you practice paying attention to this particular element; however, you will become skilled at detecting any minute variations in another person's tone. Begin by paying attention to the pitch of other people's voices as well as the clarity, resonance, tempo, volume and rhythm. It can actually be quite helpful to listen to the radio frequently, particularly talk radio. This will be a good way to gain practice.

Practice NLP Exercise

There are many NLP exercises that can be performed to give you an opportunity to hone your sensory acuity skills.

Exercise #1

In this exercise, you will come together in a group of four people. Each person within that group will provide a series of four different stories about their life. Of those stories, one will be false and three will be true. The story that is false can be placed anywhere in the sequence. Once the person has finished providing the stories, the other people in the group will attempt to determine which of the four tales was actually false based on the facial expressions and other sensory cues provided by the narrator.

Each person in the group will also make a list of the cues that they noted which help to lead to their determination regarding which of the stories was false. Everyone in the group will then discuss how their assessment of those cues helped them to reach their conclusion.

More Exercises for developing rapport and sensory acuity

The following exercises are to assist you in developing your ability to gain rapport with other people:

1. Establish rapport with as many people as you can in the coming week. For example, practice when you go into a restaurant, establish rapport with the maitre d', and with your waiter or waitress.

2. Match and mirror someone near you in a restaurant, or wherever you are. Notice if you're able to establish rapport.

3. When you're going up to a counter to purchase something, practice establishing "instant" rapport (it's possible).

4. Watch people's physiology for a whole week. For example on Monday, watch color; Tuesday, watch lower lips, etc.

To master the skill of rapport, it's important to learn the ability to gain instant rapport with anyone.

Part 9

Understanding Time Lines in NLP

The incidents that occur within our childhoods can have a profound impact on the people that we become later on in life. The patterns of behavior, thinking and emotions that we established in the past can become inappropriate in the future and can result in numerous problems in our present reality. The method of time lines helps to eradicate those old patterns which may no longer be relevant or useful in our current lives.

Using the time line process can be extremely helpful in assisting individuals in recovering from memories that are painful. Once those painful memories have been healed, the person will then be able to forgive those who hurt them and move on with their lives.

The first goal in time line is to uncover the way in which the mind actually identifies time and determines the difference between the present, the past and the future. The brain has a specific method for processing the events in our lives and for ordering all of those events in a time line.

The mind typically uses submodalities in order to determine which events occurred in the present, the past and the future. Submodaliteis are also used by the mind to determine precisely how those events were ordered. This is an entirely unconscious process. When the mind has organized the events in order they are placed on a time line. After the memories are placed on the time line, it is possible to recollect those memories.

It must be pointed out that everyone is different. While most people use visual submodalities in order to organize their memories that is not the case with everyone. Some people order their memories using auditory submodalities. Still other people use kinesthetic submodalities for ordering their memories.

Individuals who use auditory and kinesthetic submodalities typically have a more difficult time determining the difference between their memories in the present, the past and the future. Visual ordering is a much easier and more reliable method. NLP can make it possible to make a change to visual coding.

One of the most important aspects of time lining is understanding the order in which memories are stored. Many people look back over their past memories and tend to live inside those memories. They may make an attempt to change events that have already occurred, a process which can result in depression. Another common problem is living in the future. When this happens, the person may not provide any significance to events, which can result in a lack of self-motivation.

The best situation is to make sure that your future is kept firmly in front of you and the past securely behind you. This will allow you to forgive and then forget events that have already occurred while moving forward to a future that is full of possibility.

As with other forms of NLP, it is critical to make sure that you have disassociated yourself from the actual time-line. This will ensure that you do not experience any feelings that may be hurtful or negative from events that have occurred in the past.

Also, it is important to make sure that you are focusing on the images related to your memories rather than the actual content of the memories. Remember that the goal is to recall the memory, but no relive it.

Understanding your own personal time line and making sure that you are moving in the right direction can have a profound impact on your personality as well as the way in which you view life. As a result, it can become tremendously important regarding your opportunities for gaining success in the future and accomplishing your hopes, goals and dreams.

While many people remain mired hopelessly down in the past, continually reliving events that have already occurred and hoping to change their meaning in order to change their future, it is possible to make sure that you are moving in the right direction by putting those events behind you, disassociating yourself from them, removing the negativity and hurt and moving forward with your life.

Conclusion

NLP has been used around the world now for many decades and accomplished major transformations for people in all walks of life. NLP is being used successfully in many different areas such as sports, business, life coaching, medical treatments, therapy, sales, marketing, personal growth and personal development.

As NLP becomes more widely known, it is increasingly being used in business settings in order to assist individuals in overcoming the barriers that may be holding them back and preventing them from achieving their goals. This is particularly important in the sales industry, where it is critical to make sure that you can perform at absolute peak performance.

NLP is also commonly being used to eliminate negative habits and behaviors that can have a profound impact on your life and your health, including overcoming habits such as smoking.

NLP can assist you in improving any area of your life and at the same time give you the skills to influence the world around you in a positive manner.

To learn more about our NLP Trainings and watch our online NLP video training go here:

http://www.NLPUniversity.co.uk

The next few pages of this NLP section are just definitions of commonly used words within NLP. I made it available here for those of you who want to go deeper into NLP and have this as your resource when a technical word comes up, which it often does in NLP.

You can now skip to 'Section 2' to get into the five steps.

NLP Definitions

Accessing Cues	External signs that give us information about what we do inside. The signs include breathing, gestures, posture, and eye patterns.
'As-If' Frame	This is "acting as if" something were true. I.E.: Pretending that you are competent at something that you are not, like tennis. The idea is that the pretense will increase your capability.
Analogue	(As opposed to Digital) Analogue distinctions have discrete variations, as in an analogue watch.
Anchoring	The NLP Technique whereby a stimulus is linked to a response. An Anchor can be intentional or naturally occurring.
Associated	It deals with your relationship to an experience. In a memory, for example, you are associated when you are looking through your own eyes, and experiencing the auditory and kinesthetics at the same time.
Auditory	Hearing.

Backtrack	To go back and summarize or review what was previously covered, as in a meeting.
Behavior	Any external verifiable activity we engage in.
Beliefs	Generalizations we make about the world and our opinions about it.
Calibration	Usually involves the comparison between two different sets of non-verbal cues (external verifiable behavior). It allows us to distinguish another's state through non-verbal cues.
Chunking	As in thinking – moving up or down a logical level. Chunking up is moving up to a higher, more abstract level that includes the lower level. Chunking down is moving to a level, which is more specific.
Complex Equivalence	This occurs when two statements are considered to mean the same thing, E.G.: "She doesn't look at me, and that means she doesn't like me."
Congruence	When the behavior (external verifiable) matches the words the person says.
Conscious	That of which we are currently aware.
Contrastive Analysis	This is a process of analyzing two sets of SubModalities to discover the Drivers, I.E.: What makes them different. For example the difference between Ice Cream (which the client likes) and Yogurt (which the client does not like) are based on SubModality distinctions.

Content Reframe	(Also called a Meaning Reframe) Giving another meaning to a statement by recovering more content, which changes the focus, is a Content Reframe. You could ask yourself, "What else could this mean?" or "What is something you had not noticed?"
Context Reframing	Giving another meaning to a statement changing the context. You could ask yourself, "What is another context in which this behavior would be more appropriate?"
Criteria	The NLP word for values – what is important to you. (See *Time Line Therapy and the Basis of Personality*, 1988.)
Crossover Mirroring	Matching a person's external behavior with a different movement, E.G.: Moving your finger to match the client's breathing.
Deep Structure	The unconscious basis for the surface structure of a statement. Much of the deep structure is out of awareness.
Deletion	One of the three major processes (including distortion and generalization) on which the Meta Model is based. Deletion occurs when we leave out a portion of our experience.
Digital	Digital (As opposed to Analogue) Digital distinctions have distinct variations of meaning as in a Digital watch, or an "On/Off" switch.
Dissociated	It deals with your relationship to an experience. In a memory, for example,

you are dissociated when you are not looking through your own eyes, and you see your body in the picture.

Distortion	One of the three major processes (including deletion and generalization) on which the Meta Model is based. Distortion occurs when something is mistaken for that which it is not. In India there is a metaphor which explains this: A man sees a piece of rope in the road and thinks it is a dangerous snake, so he warns the village, but there is no snake.
Downtime	Downtime occurs whenever we go inside. It can occur when we go internal for a piece of information or when we get in touch with feelings. (See Up Time.)
Drivers	In SubModalities, drivers are the difference that makes the difference. Discovered through the process of Contrastive Analysis, Drivers are the critical SubModalities, and when changed tend to carry the other SubModalities with them.
Ecology	In NLP, Ecology is the study of consequences. We are interested in the results of any change that occurs. It is often useful to look at the ecology in making any change as to the consequences for self, family (or business), society and planet.
Elicitation	Inducing a state in a client, or gathering information by asking questions or observing the client's behavior.

Eye Accessing Cues	Movements of the eyes in certain directions which indicate visual, auditory or kinesthetic thinking. (See page **Error! Bookmark not defined.**.)
Epistemology	The study of knowledge or <u>how</u> we know <u>what</u> we know.
First Position	This is one of the Perceptual Positions. First Position is when you are in touch with only your own inner Model of the World.
Frame	A frame sets a context, which is a way we can make a distinction about something, as in As-If Frame, Backtrack Frame, Outcome Frame.
Future Pace	Mentally rehearsing a future result to install a recovery strategy so that the desired outcome occurs.
Generalization	One of the three major processes (including distortion and deletion) on which the Meta Model is based. Generalization occurs when one specific experience represents a whole class of experiences.
Gustatory	Taste.
Incongruence	When the behavior (external verifiable) does not match the words the person says.
Intent	The outcome of a behavior.
Internal Representations	The content of our thinking which includes Pictures, Sounds, Feelings, Tastes, Smells, and Self Talk.

Kinesthetic	This sense includes feelings, and sensations.
Law of Requisite Variety	The Law of Requisite Variety states that "In a given physical system, that part of the system with the greatest flexibility of behavior will control the system."
Leading	After pacing (matching or mirroring) a client's behavior, leading involves changing your behavior so that the other person follows your behaviors.
Lead System	This is where we go to access information. The Lead System is discovered by watching Eye Accessing Cues.
Logical Level	The level of specificity or abstraction. (E.G.: Money is a lower logical level than Prosperity.)
Logical Type	The category of information. (E.G.: Ducks are a different logical type from Cars.)
Mapping Across	Following Contrastive Analysis, Mapping Across is the SubModality process of actually changing the set of SubModalities of a certain Internal Representation to change its meaning. E.G.: Mapping the SubModalities of Ice Cream (which the client likes) over to those of Yogurt (which the client does not like) should cause the client to dislike Ice Cream.
Matching	Deliberately imitating portions of another's behavior for the purpose of increasing rapport. (E.G.: If we both

	raise our right hand, then I am matching you.)
Meaning Reframe	(Sometimes called a Content Reframe) Giving another meaning to a statement by recovering more content, which changes the focus, You could ask yourself, "What else could this mean?" or "What is something you had not noticed in this context which will change the meaning of this?"
Meta Model	Meta Model means "Over" Model. A model of language, derived from Virginia Satir that allows us to recognize deletions, generalizations and distortions in our language, and gives us questions to clarify imprecise language.
Meta Programs	These are unconscious, content-free programs we run which filter our experiences. Toward & Away From, and Matching & Mismatching are examples of Meta Programs. (See *Time Line Therapy and the Basis of Personality*, 1988)
Metaphor	A story (analogy or figure of speech) told with a purpose, which allows us to bypass the conscious resistance of the client and to have the client make connections at a deeper level.
Milton Model	The Milton Model has the opposite intent of the Meta Model (Trance), and is derived from the language patterns of Milton Erickson. The Milton Model is a series of abstract language patterns which are ambiguous so as to match our

64

client's experience and assist her in accessing unconscious resources.

Mirroring — Matching portions of another person's behavior, as in a mirror. (E.G.: If you raise your right hand, and I raise my left, then I am mirroring you.)

Mismatching — This generally relates to contradictory behavior or words, and is one of the Meta Programs.

Modal Operator — Modal Operator of Necessity relates to words, which form the rules in our lives (should, must, have to, etc.). Modal Operator of Possibility relates to words that denote that which is considered possible (can, cannot, etc.).

Model — In NLP, a Model is a description of a concept or a behavior, which includes the Strategies, Filter Patterns and Physiology so as to be able to be adopted easily.

Modeling — Modeling is the process by which all of NLP was created. In Modeling we elicit the Strategies, Filter Patterns (Beliefs and Values) and Physiology that allow someone to produce a certain behavior. Then we codify these in a series of steps designed to make the behavior easy to reproduce.

Model of the World — A person's values, beliefs and attitudes that relate to and create his or her own world.

Neuro Linguistic Programming — NLP is the study of excellence, which describes how our thinking produces our behavior, and allows us to model the

	excellence and to reproduce that behavior.
Nominalization	A process word which has been turned into a noun, often by adding "tion".
Olfactory	The sense of smell.
Outcome	Desired result.
Overlap	Using a preferred representational system to allow us to gain access to another, E.G.: "Imagine walking (preferred rep system) along the beach and hearing the birds. Now, look down at the sand and feel the cool wet sand beneath your feet."
Pacing	Pacing is matching or mirroring another person's external behavior so as to gain rapport.
Parts	Parts are a portion of the unconscious mind, which often have conflicting beliefs and values.
Parts Integration	An NLP technique, which allows us to integrate parts at the unconscious level by assisting each one to traverse logical levels (by chunking up) and to go beyond the boundaries of each to find a higher level of wholeness.
Perceptual Position	Describes our point of view in a specific situation: First Position is our own point of view. Second Position is usually someone else's point of view. Third position is the point of view of a dissociated observer.

Phonological Ambiguity	This occurs when there are two words, which sound the same but have different meanings.
Preferred Rep System	This is the representational system that someone most often uses to think, and to organize his or her experiences.
Presuppositions	Presuppositions literally means assumptions. In natural language the presuppositions are what is assumed by the sentence. They are useful in "hearing between the lines" and also for communicating to someone using assumptions that will have to be accepted by the listener so that the communication makes sense.
Presuppositions of NLP	Assumptions or convenient beliefs, which are not necessarily "true," but which if accepted and believed will change our thinking and improve our results as an NLP Practitioner.
Primary Rep System	This is how we represent our internal processing, esternally. (It is discovered by listening to Predicates and looking at Physiology.)
Punctuation Ambiguity	Ambiguity, which is created by changing the punctuation of a sentence by pausing in the wrong place, or by running-on two sentences.
Quotes	This is a Linguistic Pattern in which your message is expressed as if by someone else.
Rapport	The process of Matching or Mirroring someone so that they accept, uncritically, the suggestions you give

them. (Originally in Hypnosis 'Rapport' had a different meaning, which was, a state where the subject in Hypnosis sees, hears only the Hypnotherapist.) This is not the meaning in NLP where it relates to establishing trust and rapport between two people.

Reframing

The process of changing the frame or context of a statement to give it another meaning. In selling this process is called, "Answering Objections."

Representation

A thought in the mind which can be comprised of Visual, Auditory, Kinesthetic, Olfactory (smell), Gustatory (taste), and Auditory Digital (Self Talk).

Representational System

One of the six things you can do in your mind: Visual, Auditory, Kinesthetic, Olfactory (smell), Gustatory (taste), and Auditory Digital (Self Talk).

Resources

Resources are the means to create change within oneself or to accomplish an outcome. Resources may include certain states, adopting specific physiology, new strategies, beliefs, values or attitudes, even specific behavior.

Resourceful State

This refers to any state where a person has positive, helpful emotions and strategies available to him or her. Obviously the state implies a successful outcome

Second Position

Relating to a Perceptual Position: Second Position describes our point of view in a specific situation. Second Position is usually someone else's point

	of view. (First Position is our own point of view, Third position is the point of view of a dissociated observer.)
Sensory Acuity	This relates to observational skills. Having Sensory Acuity means that we can notice things about our client's physiology that most people would not notice.
Sensory-Based Description	Is describing someone's verifiable external behavior in a way that does not include any evaluations, but in a way that just relates the specific physiology. E.G.: "She is happy," is (in NLP terminology) an hallucination. A sensory based description would be, her lips are curved upward at the end, and her face is symmetrical.
State	Relates to our internal emotional condition. I.E.: A happy state, a sad state, a motivated state, etc. In NLP we believe that the state determines our results, and so we are careful to be in states of excellence.
Strategy	A specific sequence of internal and external representations that leads to a particular outcome.
SubModalities	These are distinctions (or subsets) that are part of each representational system that encode and give meaning to our experiences. E.G.: A picture may be in Black & White or Color, may be a Movie or a Still, may be focused or defocused – these are visual SubModalities.

69

Surface Structure	This is a linguistic term meaning the structure of our communication, which generally leaves out the completeness of the Deep Structure. The process is Deletion, Generalization and Distortion. (See also Deep Structure.)
Synesthesia	A two-step strategy, where the two steps are linked together with one usually out of awareness, as in "I want to see how I feel."
Syntactic Ambiguity	Where it is impossible to tell from the syntax of a sentence the meaning of a certain word. Often arranged by adding "ing" to a verb, as in "Hypnotizing Hypnotists can be easy."
Third Position	Relating to a Perceptual Position: Third Position describes our point of view in a specific situation. Third position is the point of view of a dissociated observer. (First Position is our own point of view, Second Position is usually someone else's point of view.)
Time Line	Our Time Line is the way we store our memories of the past, the present and the future.
Time Line Therapy™	A specific process created by Tad James, which allows the client to release negative emotions, eliminate limiting decisions and to create a positive future for himself. (See *Time Line Therapy and the Basis of Personality*, 1988.)
Trance	Any altered state. In Hypnosis it is usually characterized by inward one-pointed focus.

Unconscious	That of which you are not conscious, or which is out of awareness.
Unconscious Mind	The part of your mind that you are not conscious of … right now.
Universal Quantifiers	Words that are universal generalizations and have no referential index. Includes words such as "all", "every", and "never"
Uptime	A state where the attention is focused on the outside (as opposed to Downtime where attention is focused inward).
Values	High-level generalizations that describe that which is important to you – in NLP sometimes called criteria. (See *Time Line Therapy and the Basis of Personality*, 1988.)
Vestibular System	Having to do with the sense of balance.
Visual	Having to do with the sense of sight.
Visual Squash	(Now called Parts Integration.) An NLP technique which allows us to integrate parts at the unconscious level by assisting each one to traverse logical levels (by chunking up) and to go beyond the boundaries of each to find a higher level of wholeness.
Well Formedness	Along with the Keys to an Achievable Outcome, the Well Formedness Conditions allow us to specify outcomes that are more achievable, because the language conforms to certain rules.

SECTION II

NLPQ

$Q=$The Energy Aspect of The Human System.

This Section Covers: The Ultimate 5-Step System For Mastering The Law of Attraction, Success and Manifesting Your Goals...Every Time!

Chapter 3: Define (Step One)

This chapter will be different than the other ones. Because in this chapter I'm going to invite you watch a few videos I've produced to explain this step in detail. This is not just a book, it's a multimedia book☺.

Remember, that in this step we are defining the four most common and unconscious habits you are engaging in that is stopping your ability to master law of attraction, success and goals. We will also define the seven principles all masters are engaged in that will dramatically improve your ability. Once you know this you can stop the unconscious habits and start living the seven principles.

Enjoy the videos and transformation, go here to watch before you continue reading:

http://www.TheLimitlessProgram.com/bookbonuses

Chapter 4: Determine (Step Two)

In this chapter we are delving into step two, determine. Here I will share with you the quickest path to mastery, this goes beyond changing or fixing your beliefs, negative emotions or thoughts. These are only symptoms. In this section you'll discover what the one source of all your negatives are and determine the path you want to take to be free. The subtitle of this step could be 'What The Self Help Gurus Don't Want You To Know' as what I'm sharing here goes against what is traditionally taught and believed in the self-help industry.

Let's get started by first looking at the 'Magic Pill Syndrome'...

The Magic Pill Syndrome

Did you know that the personal development/self-help industry (adult education) is one of the major industries in the world? Do you know why? Because, after 25 years' experience in the industry, as a participant/seeker and then as a coach/teacher, I discovered that everyone is looking for the Magic Pill.

You know what I'm talking about, 'the pill' that will take all your problems, obstacles, pains and suffering away. 'The pill' that will take away your procrastination, the habit of not following through and getting distracted.

"The pill' that will make you happy all the time, with unlimited energy, wake up early and go to bed late. The pill that will get you stop eating the chocolate cake you know you shouldn't eat, the pill that will make your spouse finally get sane and be exactly as the image you have of them instead of loving them for who they are.

You know what pill I'm talking about, don't you? Haven't we all been there, seeking the magic pill that will change everything?

I know I have, been going to seminar after seminar, reading book after book. Maybe the next seminar will have the answer (magic pill), maybe the next book will have the solution to all my problems.

Guess what, after a being in the industry for over 25 years I can now tell you with absolute certainty that there isn't any Magic Pill out there!

And if you are a committed and if you're being honest with yourself you know this is true. You know that even when you've tried this technique or that process or this method you didn't end up having a stable, permanent and lasting change.

You didn't end up experiencing stable joy, happiness and unconditional love. You didn't achieve the constant motivation and peace of running your business to even greater heights. This is what makes this industry one of the most profitable and lucrative industries you can get into.

75

Because we are still out there seeking and wanting The Answer, The Magic Pill.

This industry thrives on you looking for the Magic Pill. It loves when you spend more money and more time to find the answer. And the company that's promoting the answers always have another product, program or teacher that will definitely give you the answer.

Do you know why you can't find the answer? Do you know why they can't find the answer?

The Answer Doesn't 'Lie' There

Here are two short answers and then we will explore this more in depth as we continue.

1. Most teachers, trainers, life coaches, students are looking for the answer in a place where only temporary change can happen. You see anytime you are trying to change, fix or improve yourself you are reinforcing what you are trying to change on an unconscious level.

Metaphorically speaking say you have a pen in your hand, and you want to change, fix or improve that pen. In order to change the pen you have to have the pen there in order to change it. Hence every time you are trying to change it you are reinforcing the pen being in your hand. You are giving the pen power, the fuel it needs to survive.

This would be like running west looking for a sunset, you could be running all your life and never find it

2. The assumption, or what we presuppose, in our search for answers and solutions is coming from a place that doesn't produce the result we want and in some cases produces a false positive illusion of change. Instead the traditional approach to change or self-improvement reinforces the problem we are trying to change or fix.

This would be like making calculations on a calculator where every time you press '5' you get '2' on the screen. It doesn't matter how many calculations we make, how nice they sound or for how long we are going to calculate, in the final analysis our calculations will always be false. And hence our experience if we are living those 'calculations' must be false.

The following will make the two above answers be clearer. When we say:

- 'I want to change my negative emotion'
- "I don't like this anger, I want to get rid of it"
- "I just want to be happy"
- "I want to be better"

• "If I could only change my feelings about…"

• "I want change my limiting belief to something empowering"

• "I want to improve myself"

Who is this "I"? What is this "I"? Who is my-'self? Traditionally when people are talking about change or self-improvement, they are referring to the Self/the 'I'. The self is your 'I' dentity your personality. Some call it 'ego'. Some call it 'your psychology'.

Let's define this as your Self.

The Creation of Self and Your reality – The 'I'

The purpose of The Self is too organize your reality so you can survive and experience this world. Why? Because we are bombarded with 4 billion bits of information per second, and our nervous system can't handle that.

However our nervous system is very intelligent and will delete, distort and generalize these 4 billion bits into only 2000 bits. That is 0.000054% of the 4 billion bits. The reason the nervous system does this because it wants to take the 4 billion bits which is called chaos and put it into order.

We could then say that the purpose of the nervous system is to organize chaos into order for optimum survival.

The 0.00054% or 2000 bits that we take from the 4 billion is what we call The Self. That is what you call your reality. That is what you call your life, 0.00054%. This is what we get into arguments for, this is what we kill other people for and this is what we sometimes have grief over, 0.000054% of reality which you call your reality. This is The 'I'.

Is there something greater outside this 'I'? Is it possible to experience more happiness and joy outside the prison of the 'I'? What's beyond The Self? The Answer to all these questions are covered as you read on. Let's explore The Self a bit more…

The Self (The 'I') consists of your memories, values' beliefs, attitudes and emotions etc.

Your Memories are all the experiences you had throughout your life stored in your mind. The purpose of your memories is twofold:

1.	From biological perspective your memories help you survive in the world. E.g. The first time you burnt yourself on the stove is recorded as memory so next time you see it you avoid it.

2.	From an evolutionary perspective your memories serves as your teacher or guide, to make you evolve from a Human to a Being.

Your memories are there to guide you so you can evolve beyond your past experiences and transcend your old patterns of interacting with the world.

E.g. say someone was in a past relationship where they were doing everything to please their partner, after a while the partner got bored and left the relationship. The person who was left behind will most likely be feeling angry, sad, betrayed, hurt and unworthy. They might have an internal dialogue similar to this one "How could he leave me? I did everything for him. I always put him first. He doesn't understand how much I love him. How could he do this to me? I hope I never see him again." Now the purpose of that event, which later will be a memory is to make you evolve. However this gets forgotten because all memories are usually associated with emotions, and emotions are there to code the memory for you.

Hence if 'painful' emotions are associated to that memory you will avoid anything that's similar to that memory and if it's a 'pleasure' emotion you will want anything that's similar to that memory.

Another way of stating this would be that anything that approximates your 'positive' or 'negative' memory in your present time environment, will make you move towards it or away from it, whatever that 'it' is in your environment.

That's why many people in relationships are not in a relationship with their partners, they're in relationship with an image (for example an intense pleasurable memory from teenage years) that they now want to experience again and hoping that there partner will live up to that image.

Instead of getting bogged down in the emotions of the memory, step back and take the learning's from that memory. The learning from the example above could be for that person to realize that their underlying belief is that they perceive themselves as unworthy. And when that person can fully own that belief and then transcend that belief, this person is now free to have their next experience to evolve from Human to Being. If this doesn't happen the person will keep attracting the same relationship over and over again, the only difference is the faces they meet, and this will continue until they do own it and transcend it.

Your Values are what is important to you in life, health, relationships etc. If I asked you what's important to you in health you might say clarity or energy. Then that would be some of your values in the area of health. Your values are born out of your perceived voids in your life. If I have a perceived lack of health or wellbeing then I will most likely have that as a value in the area of health. If I have a perceived lack of money, then making money might be a value (of high importance) in my life. If I feel like I'm lacking love, finding love will be a high value in my life.

Your Beliefs are what you believe is true about yourself, your world, people, places, things and events. And when you decide consciously or unconsciously what is a true, then that decision will become your filter for how you perceive the world or your self.

E.g. If when I was in high school I failed a few times in the math's class, I could have decided that "maths is tough" or "I'm not good at maths". Now, ten years later someone

offers me a job that requires some ability to work with numbers, I might turn it down because of my old belief of "I'm not good with math's". Is it true that I wasn't good with math's? No.

With more knowledge and training I would be very good at math's. However as soon as I decided

"I'm not good with math's" I immediately shut off from any other possibility. And from then on I'm walking through the world as if it's true. A belief is a little bit like colored lenses. If you have a yellow colored lens when you walk through the world, then all you will see is yellow regardless of what's really there. Masters transcend their beliefs and therefore their limitations. Remember instead of looking at beliefs as something that is true, what would happen if you started to look at your beliefs and ask yourself "Is this belief making me limited or unlimited?".

What colored lenses are you wearing that might be limiting you?

Your attitude is collection of emotions you have combined in a certain way which then becomes an attitude. E.g. a mix of anger, sadness and frustration might lead to an attitude of hostility. A mix of joy, bliss and happiness might lead to an attitude of warmth.

Your emotions are labels you put on the somatic sensations we experience in our physiology. Some sensations we have learned throughout our lives is called anger. Now the challenge with emotions is that so many people are afraid of them. We have learned e.g. that this sensation in my stomach and throat means I'm sad (label) and being sad is bad (evaluation) and I don't want to be sad(preference).

This way we are resisting the sensations we labelled bad and hence anything you resist will persist. What do most people do when they experience an emotion? They either express it e.g. yell at someone or suppress e.g. have a drink. Neither of these two ways will rarely evolve you nor free you from the pain you're trying to avoid. Keep in mind that emotions are labels and then we attach meanings to these labels, and that's what usually is causing the perceived suffering people experience when it comes to emotions.

What would happen if you took away the labels and meanings you associated with your emotions? What if you just stripped it all away and all that was left was the sensation in your body? Another thing you can do next time you feel angry or sad, decide to be joyful about your anger or sadness. Do it, be joyfully angry or joyfully sad. Notice what happens when you do that.

Your Self (The 'I') also consists of your conscious mind (the one that's analyzing if what you're reading at this moment makes sense or not) and your unconscious mind (which makes you breath right now without you having to think about it, it happens all by itself). Simplified you I would say that the majority (99%) of the trainers, seminar leaders, life coaches out there today are working with the Self. This is the industry standard when it comes to change and self-improvement; we are assuming that this, what we just described above, is the self. And that in it-self is where the main problem lies.

We can go to a self-help program and change our limiting belief "I have to have money to make money" to an empowering belief "I only have to have a great idea to make money", now did we really make a change here? Or we can release our negative emotion such as anger from the past? However did we really make a change here? Or we can learn to set goals and manage our states.

But what really happened here? Let's see....

How the Self is really constructed and why the above approaches to change is dealing with the symptoms and not the cause.

When we delve deeper into the Self (The 'I'), you'll find that The Self is actually compromised of two facets:

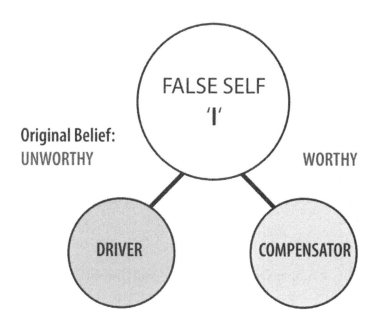

The two facets are as illustrated above is what we call the Driver and then you have the Compensator.

What is the Driver and the Compensator:

• **The Driver** is your first conclusion or belief about yourself which then organizes your whole psychology and thus creates The Self (The 'I') based on that conclusion. We call that first conclusion your Original Belief or Original Self- Image. There are about 9 major conclusions that most people tend to make.

These conclusions are adopted or created for most people as a pre-verbal cognition when we are between 5 -12 months old and then reinforced during our Imprint Period up until approx. 7 years old.

An example of an Original Belief or Conclusion would be as above "I am unworthy" and another one would be "I am inadequate". Now, this will be the foundational viewpoint of how you view your life, this is your first conclusion that you will act on unconsciously. This is the first lens you start to wear and then forgot you put on in the first place. Again this first conclusion or original belief is what we call the Driver. The problem with the Driver is that most of us are really unconscious about its existence. And here's where the Compensator comes in…

• **The Compensator** is the way you unconsciously trying to overcome, heal, get rid of or change your Driver. The Compensator will do anything in its power to ensure that you never have to experience the pain of your Driver. So, if my Driver is "I am unworthy" my Compensator will develop beliefs, values and goals so I can heal, overcome, hide, change or get rid of my Driver. With the above illustrated example my Compensator will go out in the world with the mission of being "Worthy" (due to the Driver is 'Unworthy').

That might mean having two doctor degrees, a seven figure income, three luxury cars, and 0.002% body fat and when I have all of that then I can feel worthy, or when I have achieved all of that then other people can see how worthy I am.

This might take another turn and we project our Driver "I am unworthy" on to other people so then they become "unworthy" and we need to 'fix' them so we can feel worthy. We might even do this in our most intimate relationships. Our spouse becomes 'unworthy' and then we attempt (I used attempt deliberately, cause we all know how fatal it is trying to change your spouse☺), to change fix or improve them to so we can feel worthy. Or we might even get into a relationship with someone who is successful (whatever that means to you) in other people's eyes, because then they can see how worthy I am.

Now, this gives you an idea of how the Self (The 'I') is really constructed. **Most of the personal development programs and psychology are trying to change, fix or improve your Compensator (e.g. changing beliefs or visualizing), and every attempt to do so is only reinforcing the Driver.**

Why?

1.   Because the Driver is the first conclusion you made and hence is the strongest

2.   The Compensator is born out of the Driver

3.   The Driver and The Compensator is actually the same holographic unit, you can't have one without the other.

Here are some examples of common Drivers and Compensators:

Driver	Compensator
I am imperfect. There must be something wrong. with me .	Prove there is not something wrong with me by being perfect or being with someone who is perfect.
I am worthless, or have no value.	Prove I am not worthless by proving I am worthy.
I can't do anything.	Proving I can do anything by achieving and over-do.
I am inadequate.	Proving I am not inadequate, by proving adequacy.
I do not exist, I am non-existent.	Prove existence.
I am alone.	Trying to connect, over-connecting.
I am incomplete.	Prove I am complete through people or experiences.
I am powerless.	Prove how powerful I am.
I am unlovable.	Proving I am lovable by being extra-loving.
I am out of control.	Prove I have control by trying to control self/others.
I am crazy.	Proving I am healthy.
I am not safe.	Prove I am safe by creating safety for self and others, so they create safety for me.
I am not supported.	Prove I am supported by creating support for self and others, so they support me.

"Anything you are trying to change, fix, improve or 'get rid of' is reinforcing the very problem you are trying to overcome"

Any attempt to change, fix, improve or 'get rid of' the Driver is reinforcing the Driver, in fact the very act of wanting to change, fix or improve is born out of the Driver at an unconscious level with the purpose to survive. Because you'll always need the Driver there in order to fix it or heal it.

This is why you can never find <u>The Answer</u> and this is why people are going to program after program, seminar after seminar, reading book after book.

So, what is the way out?

The first step is to really realize and know, that there's nothing you need to change, fix or improve.

And that the very act of doing that is resisting your reality and hence your reality as you experience it today will persist.

Sometimes when I raise this concept, I get the following comments from people:

"Yes, that's so true" "I never thought about it that way" "But I do want a better life" "I want to earn millions of dollars" "And I do want to be a better husband or wife" "I definitely want to get rid of the pain (e.g. guilt, anxiety etc.)"

"You can have all you desire, but not from the same level of mind that wants it. Because the level of mind that wants it is resisting what is and hence keeps creating the very thing it doesn't want"

What is the way out? If it's not fixing, improving or changing things, then what is it?

Before we go onto answer that question, let's look at….

The Two Things That Keeps You Trapped and Limited in Your Driver-Compensator Psychology.

The answer here will address <u>what not to do</u> (we have touched on them earlier but it's worth going through it again in the context of the driver-compensator psychology).

90

There are two things people tend to do that keeps them trapped in their minds:

1.   **Analyzing** – people tend analyze everything. I've noticed a direct relation between how your level of analyzing is corresponding to your level of discomfort. The more we analyze the more we tend to feel discomfort (e.g. anger, frustration, sadness etc.). Many times the analyzing is a re-enactment of your Driver. The question that drives the analyzing is: Why?

It's like if a friend comes over and says "I'm depressed" what do most of us do, we ask the question "Why?" Now, think about this, what kind of effect does this question really create?

It makes us focus on the story of why we are depressed, hence creating more of what? Yes, that's right, more depression " I'm depressed because I didn't get the results I wanted "or "I'm depressed because she didn't call me for over two months, that must mean she doesn't love me".

Have you ever experienced something like this? I'm sure you have. Did you notice that both answers to the questions of why was determined by something outside of themselves. They got depressed about some external factor which means that they were also putting their power of how they feel on something outside themselves. Is there a better way than that?

91

When we stop analyzing we actually tap into more power and clarity within ourselves and from there we can experience freedom from what the analyzing is trying to overcome, e.g. feeling unworthy or feeling inadequate etc.

Your first step could be that from now on decide not to analyze. Do it only for a few minutes and notice what happens…

Analyzing was the first thing that got us trapped and here's the second one…

2. **Resisting** – we tend to resist what is happening in our world. In Buddhism they say that suffering is caused not by the event itself but from our resistance to that event. Another simple example would be that something triggers your anger, now the anger in itself usually wouldn't create sustained suffering. However now that you're experiencing anger, the next thing you do is to be frustrated about your anger ("Here I go again, I'm angry, even though I promised I wouldn't be), and then you get sad ("Can't I ever get it right, does it always have to be this way") about your frustration about your anger. This is resisting the initial experience of anger. What would happen if you stopped resisting the anger in that situation and just be in acceptance of it? What would happen if you stopped resisting what is?

This doesn't mean that if someone is being rude to you by, e.g. always putting you down or invalidating you in front of everyone in a meeting at work, and you respond "Yes, that's okay, I'm not going to resist this. I'll just accept 100% what he/she is doing" and then leave it at that. That's not what I mean. What I do suggest is that instead of reacting to the situation by resisting it, which gives birth to unresourceful emotions and thoughts which drains you of power to handle the situation effectively, you accept what is and respond from the power of who you really with all resources available to you. You'll be amazed of what happens. This might not make 100% sense yet, but as you practice it in your own life you will notice the difference. WARNING! Don't try this at home or in your life, you can experience serious joy and happiness☺

Who is this Power and You beyond your-Self?

In Quantum Physics they talk about that "Reality is Observer Created, Without Any Observer There's No Reality".

What does that mean? Who is the Observer they are talking about? Is there a difference between you (The False Self) and the Observer (The Limitless YOU)? Let's look at the model below:

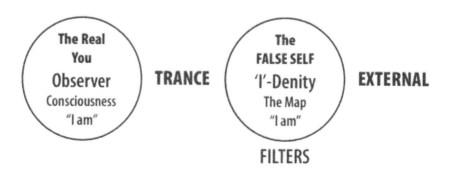

The Real You (The Limitless You) is the Observer, in spiritual traditions it has been called the "I Am", Being or Essence. Whatever you call it this is who YOU REALLY ARE, this is The Real You.

Now, most of us have forgotten that and are in trance with our Self's, our 'I'- dentities, you could say we are hypnotized by our own thoughts and act as if that is who you are.

However the truth is you are not the False Self (Driver – Compensator with its limiting beliefs, negative emotions, thoughts, behaviors and habits).

The Limitless You is where you have all your power, abilities, strength and life force to handle everything, create anything, connecting with your true purpose and fulfilment. Here is where you can experience the freedom that most people only dream of and this is where you'll experience immense joy, peace, happiness and unconditional love.

The False Self is currently creating your reality and this is why The Law of Attraction doesn't work in the way people are intending as many people are trying to attract through the limitations of the False Self.

As you can see in the model below when you are tapping into The Limitless You all Possibilities Exist (Quantum Physics calls this Superposition), All Waves of Possibilities Exist. From this space you can Be and Do and Have whatever you decide. It's the ultimate cause-point instead of being under the effect of the False Self with all its limitations.

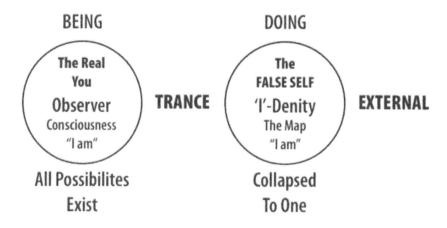

What's stopping you from tapping into the power you really are is:

• Your attachments and aversions to your external world (e.g. status, house, cars, looks, people, places, things, events etc.)

• Your addictions to having the same emotional feelings on a consistent basis (e.g. you could be addicted to creating a drama with your spouse every week, so you push him/her away by withdrawing your affection/love and hence they might push you away as a reaction to that, and then you'll feel rejected and unloved by their reaction. And voila' you fulfilled your addiction of feeling rejected or unloved. This is mostly unconscious for people. We have amnesia around it, and can't even see it when it's being pointed out by someone else. The games we play to be right and protect our Driver)☺.

• The tendency to be obsessive-compulsive about changing, fixing, improving ourselves.

Really realize and know, that there's nothing you need to change, fix or improve. And that the very act of doing that is the act of resisting your current reality which in turn creates a persisting reality you don't want to experience.

The Big Stop From Tapping Into Your Full Power and Potential

The default use of language and words is stopping you from realizing your full power.

Without language and words you wouldn't be able to have thoughts. Without thoughts you wouldn't be able to have so called "problems". I usually challenge the participants in my seminars by asking them to contemplate the following:

Can a problem (disregarding the fight/flight/freeze responses to protect us as an organism) exist without thoughts, words or language?

Can you feel sad or feel betrayed without language or words? My conclusion is you can't.

In order to feel sad you have to have a word for the sensation labelled sadness and then you have to associate meanings (thoughts) about sadness and then this together will create an experience which we could judge as being a 'good' or 'bad' experience (by use of language). Hence we could have a potential problem. But without any words or language that problem wouldn't exist.

Why is this?

Because in order to hear anything anyone says and create an understanding of what they are communicating and for us to able to communicate, we're going through a process called transduction.

When you hear someone talk, what you are doing is interpreting sound waves that are hitting your ears, these sound waves are then being sent to your brain which in turn translates the sound waves into words. These words are being translated into meanings which you then evaluate as being a potential pain or pleasure. This means that you can never hear what someone else is saying all you're hearing is what you're brain has been imprinted to hear through your conditioning.

Words play a big role in keeping us limited in the Self (The 'I'). Because we have given words power, we are acting as if the word is the thing it's supposed to designate. As Alfred Korzybski, the father of General Semantics, said: "The Map is not The Territory". The word is not the thing it's supposed to designate.

The word enlightment is not enlightment. It is only a description of an experience that we culturally have decided to mean a certain thing. But the word enlightment doesn't have any meaning outside that context, cultural agreement or system. You can't be enlightened, because it's a word. You can have the experience of something called enlightment, but in order to get there you have let go of the boundaries and limitations that words sometimes can put on an experiences.

To be in your full power, potential and ability, you have to go beyond words and thoughts, which is stepping outside your 'I'-dentity (false self). You have to be in the awareness outside of thoughts, associations, memories, emotions and meanings that is born out of the false self, you are now being present. This is where you're true power is and this where you can start manifesting your ultimate reality.

These are the five things we do with words and thoughts that keeps us in The False Self (The 'I'):

• **Labelling** – is the first step in the process of creating your experiences in the Self. Something is happening in your body or in your external environment. E.g. Your spouse makes a squinted face and you label that as she is being angry.

• **Judging** – the second step is judging what you just labelled. E.g. you judge your spouse being angry as she doesn't like you.

• **Evaluate** – the thirds step is you evaluate what you judged. E.g. if she doesn't like me than maybe she'll stop loving me.

• **Significance** – the fourth step is put significance on your evaluation. E.g. If she doesn't love me, than I'm unlovable.

• **Preference** – the fifth step is to have a preference about your evaluations. E.g. I don't want to feel unlovable. And as we said before anything resisted will persist.

The best thing you can do to tap into your power and step outside the False Self is to stop judging, evaluating, having significances and preferences.

I call the process above, JESPing. When you stop JESPing you will be free and I think you'll notice that a lot of your so called problems will disappear.

Five Things You Can Do Step Outside the Self and Be In Your Power, Be The Real You

1.   <u>Stop Analyzing</u> – stop the habit of asking why. Why didn't he call me? Did I do something wrong? Why am I acting this way? What's wrong with me? All this is analyzing.

2.   100% Acceptance – start having 100% acceptance of everything that is happening in your life. Have 100% acceptance of yourself, your world, of people, places, things and events in your life. Have 100% acceptance of what is.

3.   Stop resisting emotions – start to play with your emotions by taking your awareness away from the story (your reason) for having the emotion and just watch the emotion (sensation that you labelled) for what it is. Watch it without wanting to change it, fix it or getting rid of it. This will free you, give it a go and experience it for yourself.

4.   Stop JESPing - Stop judging, evaluating, having significance or preference you thoughts or emotions.

5.   Be present – be present in the now moment without any thoughts, associations, memories, emotions or agendas. You can do this easily by taking your focus away from the story you're running in your head and put that focus on the sensations you're feeling inside your body. Have you ever felt the sensation you have in your right hand in this now moment? Go ahead do it now and notice what happens when all your awareness is there. You also put all your awareness on the space between your breaths. Do it now. Remember reading about all of this is nice intellectual stimulation, but intellectual stimulation is not necessarily going to change your life. However if you take your focus away from the story in your head and put that focus on the space between your breaths, you'll might discover something really powerful. Do this exercise for ten minutes and notice the change.

The Solution To It All

Before we continue…the effective way to let go of the False Self (driver-compensator psychology with all the negative beliefs, emotions, thoughts, habits and behaviors) which is the symptom is to work with what I call the Master Programs and Charges which are the glue that holds the False Self together.

It's the Master Programs and Charges that are the cause of all your limitations, barriers, stops and obstacles, and once you have addressed them you are free.

A Charge is an energy packet which holds your negative beliefs, emotions, thoughts, habits and limitations in place regarding your view of yourself, the world, people, places, things, situations, events and capabilities. In one word it's the false self.

The Master Programs is the fundamental way in which our false self is acting, unconsciously, with ourselves and the world. All our negative behaviors, emotions and thoughts are derived from our master programs. Our three master programs are:

- Seeking approval

- Seeking control

- Seeking security or survival

The best way to release the false self is to release your foundational charges and master programs.

In our next chapter I'm going to share with you one tool you can start using to release your negatives and the false self. By no means is the next chapter the full set of tools and processes I use to assist people. However it is the easiest tool to share in the context of a book and without additional knowledge (otherwise this book could be over 500 pages and I'm not sure how many would read that)☺.

This tool is also proven extremely effective and fast in producing results. Hence I want to share it with you now as this can have major positive effects in your life. This tool is also proven to eliminate negative emotions and habits in minutes.

Before we go into our next chapter let's have look and see how all of this fits in with The Law Of Attraction…

The Law of Attraction - BE DO HAVE

In this section we will explore how The Law of Attraction really works, how it can work for you and why so many keep attracting the same reality over and over again, even though they are utilizing the principles of The Law of Attraction.

To understand this we will start with the principle that everything in your life and everything in this universe has a frequency, it has a certain vibration.

For example your computer screen has a certain frequency, when you make a call on your mobile phone that call has a different frequency, the light from your lamp has frequency, your radio receives in the hertzian frequency, whilst your microwave is using infra-red frequency, even your thoughts and emotions has a certain frequency. This is important, because this is what you are attracting today into your life, you are attracting anything that is frequency specific to who you are being (for majority of the population that is the frequency of their False Self).

Let's say I take two tuning forks, tuning fork A and tuning fork B and put them in different locations in the room. Now, if I hit tuning fork A and A starts to vibrate and create a sound, guess what happens to tuning fork B. Without touching it, tuning fork B will start to vibrate and create a sound similar to A.

Why?

Because A was in a certain frequency or vibration and B due to the law of harmony had no choice other than to start vibrating at the same level. You have heard about people who can scream and through the frequency of their sound waves they break glass or porcelain. This is how powerful and real the power of frequency is.

Metaphorically who you are being today is tuning fork A (which is having a specific frequency) and will attract tuning fork B (which is in the same frequency to you) into your reality. Earlier we said your thoughts, emotions and attitudes (collective name is your charges as described earlier) have a certain frequency, so if you're in an angry state you'll end up attracting more anger into your life. Because that is what is frequency specific to you .

The Law of Attraction then suggests that we focus our thoughts and feelings on what we want to have in our life to the exclusion of anything else. The challenge here is that what gets attracted for most people is the same old reality over and over again, and the second challenge is for most people it's not working to the extent that they expected.

This is happening due to the False Self, which is mostly unconscious and most of the time in a negative frequency (the underlying Driver – e.g. 'I m unworthy').

What most people are doing is to attract and focus their new reality through the conscious mind (The Compensator – e.g. 'Im worthy') and are forgetting that at the same time their unconscious mind (The Driver – e.g. 'Im unworthy') is also attracting what is frequency specific to that mind, and since both parts of the False Self exists due to the negative conclusion (e.g. im unworthy) this is the frequency that will be attracted.

This is what I call manifesting reality through conditioning, we are attracting through the conditioning of our False Self.

To fully apply the principles of The Law of Attraction we have to let go of our False Self (the charges and the master programs), because when you do that, you are letting go of the old programs and patterns that you are running unconsciously. As said before these old programs are the source of you keep attracting the old into your life. That's why people are having the same experiences in life but it might show up in different forms e.g. different partners but same scenarios.

When you are letting go of the False Self you are now being The Limitless You (The Observer in Quantum Physics) and from here you can now make your intention (whatever it is you desire to experience in your life) the Law and it will manifest in your life.

Now that you come this far and learned some new knowledge, my recommendation is to ask yourself:

1. 'How can I apply what I have learnt here to my life?'

2. 'What new decisions can I make with this new understanding of myself and life?'

3. 'What is one thing I can do right now that will move me forward to my goals and ultimate life?'

If you want to learn more about the false self, the charges and master program, please join the free bonus webinar you got as part of purchasing this book, go here now:

http://www.LifeImprovementEvents.com

As I said before in our next chapter I'm going to share with you one of the tools so you can start using it to release your negatives and the false self.

This tool is also proven extremely effective and fast in producing results. Hence I want to share it with you now as this can have major positive effects in your life. This tool is also proven to eliminate negative emotions and habits in minutes.

Let s get started…

Chapter 5: DELETE (Step Three)

Congratulations for coming this far and taking the time to learn the principles that will transform your life. As you know many people want to transform their lives, they talk about it but few actually are taking action and doing something about it. Hence I want to acknowledge you for getting this far. Now...

Let's continue our journey by applying one of the most effective tools for letting go of negative emotions, thoughts and habits. You'll be learning this tool in the context of abundance as this is usually one of the most charged areas in most people's lives. However the exact techniques you'll get here can be used to any area of life.

The subtitle of this chapter could be: How To Get Everything You've Ever Wanted in Life and More

EFT – Tapping Into Abundance

Removing the Emotional Blocks to Financial Success

"The only place where success comes before work is in the dictionary." – Vidal Sassoon

Does the perfect financial situation seem just out of reach? Are you struggling to pay the bills each month? Do you feel like somehow you and money just weren't meant to be a happy couple?

Whether you want to watch your new business prosper and start earning you money, or you just need to keep your head above water and manage your debts, money woes are the biggest problems we face. But what we don't realize is that the real problem isn't "out there" but inside. It's your limiting beliefs that stop you from creating the abundance you need.

The secret to creating wealth is not to gain anything but to lose. We need to lose the negative thought and behavior patterns which hold us back. When released from these self-sabotaging bad habits, you're then free to do whatever needs to be done to make prosperity happen in your life.

It's harder than you think to stop these bad habits, but there's a method that can work wonders – Emotional Freedom Techniques, also known as EFT. It uses meridian tapping, a practice based on acupressure and traditional Chinese medicine, along with positive affirmations to break the stranglehold negativity has on you.

The key is the 'F' in EFT – freedom. This method sets you free, releasing you from your negative emotional blocks.

The chapter you're reading now will explain to you what EFT is and how you can use this powerful healing strategy to release the blocks standing between you and your prosperity. You'll learn hands-on how to do it and ideas for customizing its methods for you.

You'll learn:

• How truly damaging negative thought patterns are to your life

• How to identify and tackle these patterns

• The basics of EFT and how it can be applied to your money problems

• Step-by-step how to create an effective tapping sequence

• Ideas on how to refine your sequence if you're not getting the results you want

• Advanced techniques to help you achieve even more prosperity

It may be hard to believe that you're going to be living in prosperity and abundance, but you have already taken the first step. EFT is amazingly simple and results are fast. The first step you have taken is the hardest. It gets much easier from here!

An Introduction to EFT

First of all, let's give EFT an official definition - EFT is a psychological acupressure technique that helps you deal with your emotions in our modern hyper-tense world.

Let's take a closer look. Acupressure means acupuncture and other techniques used in traditional Chinese medicine to get your energy flowing right. We'll discuss that in more detail below.

What do I mean by hyper-tense? It means that human beings have never lived in such a stressful environment as they do today. The tigers and woolly mammoths that chased our ancient hunter-gatherer ancestors around were nothing compared to traffic jams, evil bosses, deadlines and the impossible pits of debt we face today.

Because of this modern-day madness, human beings are plagued by steadily increasing levels of mental illnesses. Anxiety, depression and stress-related illnesses are at an epidemic rate. High rates of chronic diseases such as heart disease and cancer are also related to these astronomic stress levels.

We live in an anxious age and it makes us all a little sick. EFT is a way to naturally alleviate the anxieties ailing us.

The Goal of EFT

The goal of EFT is to help you stay calm and balanced in the face of adversity. When you're stuck in a traffic jam and the cars aren't moving, you feel like smacking your head against the windshield until one or the other breaks. EFT allows you to employ simple techniques with no tools or special skills necessary to suddenly release your anger and frustration and better again.

EFT has been found to provide treatment for a wide range of ailments including chronic pain, post-traumatic stress disorder, anxiety, depression, obsessive-compulsive disorder, addictions and even physical ailments.

However, EFT isn't just for people who are ill or depressed. It's a tool people can use to overcome the obstacles keeping them from their dreams and fortunes. In this book, you're going to learn how to use EFT to enhance your life by removing negative blocks that keep you from reaching your financial goals and creating abundance in your life.

Where Does EFT Come From?

"You've done it before and you can do it now. See the positive possibilities. Redirect the substantial energy of your frustration and turn it into positive, effective, unstoppable determination." - Ralph Marston

EFT is a treatment for the modern age but its roots are in ancient practices. It's an interdisciplinary field that combines psychology, neuroscience, natural healing, and electromagnetic energy flow techniques. It's similar to hypnosis, meditation and acupressure.

The roots of EFT are in the ancient Chinese practice of acupuncture which involves placing needles in strategic locations on the body in order to remove blockages of energy. The word for energy in Chinese is "qi" (pronounced 'chee').

Energy flows through the body along "meridians." There are key points where meridians meet. You can think of them as highway intersections. Picture a busy intersection where there's a traffic jam and cars aren't moving. According to Chinese medicinal practices, this is the cause of your ailments – the energy gets bunched up at these intersection points. Needles are inserted at these points and the flow is released.

If getting poked by needles isn't your idea of a therapeutic good time, don't worry – there are other techniques employed in Chinese medicine. Some involve burning your skin at these key points or zapping you with electricity.

Still doesn't sound like fun? Well, EFT is a simpler version that's non-invasive, easy to learn, and requires no tools or expertise. Instead of poking, burning or zapping, you tap these points with your fingertips and this provides the relief you need.

The Negative Thoughts that Hold You Back

"Have no fear of perfection - you'll never reach it."

—Salvador Dalí

Chinese medicine practitioners use acupressure (a variety of treatments that include acupuncture) to treat physical and mental ailments. With modern-day EFT, we go after negative patterns of thought.

A person who wants to lose weight would tap and focus on the negative feelings that make them overeat. If you were trying to overcome a dependence on alcohol, you would first identify the thoughts that drive you to drink.

In the same way, negative thoughts are holding you back from achieving your financial goals. What's scary is that you may not even know they're there.

Think for a minute and you may know exactly which negative thoughts about money are holding you back. This means they're at the conscious level. But more often, they're at the subconscious level where they're hidden from view. If this is the case, it may take some tapping to bring them out.

When you use EFT for financial success, you start by identifying these negative thoughts. Then, you work on releasing them as you tap.

Does EFT Really Work?

"Faith is taking the first step even when you don't see the whole staircase." ~ Martin Luther King, Jr.

The idea of qi, or life energy, flowing through the body is a new one for the West, but not other cultures. Since it's a new idea, many people are skeptical of it. Their chief argument is that there is no scientific evidence to support that acupressure works. All we have to go on are the testimonials of those who have undergone this type of therapy.

EFT relies on knowledge of electromagnetic energy, which is not well understood by science. As more research is done, it may come to be more widely accepted. But in non-Western cultures, it's taken as fact that these energies are flowing through the body and having a great effect on our lives. It may be a matter of western medicine "catching up," just like it has done with natural remedies and other alternative health practices.

Although there's no scientific evidence to support EFT's healing claims, it's now widely used by medical practitioners and there's one simple reason – it works. EFT first gained widespread attention in the 1990s when it was used to treat returning soldiers with post-traumatic stress syndrome. Therapists now use the technique to treat everything from migraine headaches to drug addiction.

Some people are skeptical because it just looks funny. You can see videos of people tapping their faces and mumbling to themselves, and if the description below didn't tell you that this is EFT, you'd think they were crazy! But remember that people said the same thing about yoga, affirmations, acupuncture and meditation, all of which are fairly common today.

The Best Benefit of EFT

The best benefit EFT has to offer is that it's simple and it can be learned in just a few minutes. By the time you finish this book, you'll be ready to get started. And best of all, results can be instantaneous. If you work EFT into your regular daily routine and practice it over the long-term, the results can be life-changing.

And one more benefit is that you have got nothing to lose. There are no side effects and the worst that can happen is that it won't work for you.

Tackling Your Negative Thoughts

"I don't pray for God to take my problems away, I pray only for God to give me the strength to go through them."

~ Jose Lozano

EFT consists of two components – meridian tapping and positive affirmations. While you tap, you repeat your affirmations to yourself. This has a powerful effect on your mind. The affirmation is working its magic while the tapping releases your energies from their blockages.

The first step is to identify the negative thoughts with which you're sabotaging yourself. This is called your "target."

"Sabotage" is a strong word. Why on earth would anybody actively prevent themselves from getting whatever they want out of life? If you want it, why can't you just get it?

The reason is you developed bad habits of thinking and they're usually buried in your subconscious. This means you can't access or change them (not easily, anyway – methods such as hypnosis must be used).

We are created with ingredients we didn't choose. In our early lives, we are shaped by processes we can't control. As a result, we grow up to become adults that are not always what we'd like to be.

You learned to cling to your pain, anger, frustration or self-doubt because it's comfortable for you. Holding to that self-doubt is a better option than the alternative – the unknown. Clinging to these negative thoughts is the basis of self-sabotage.

Here's an example – imagine that your car is cluttered. You open the door and an old Starbucks cup falls out. Without thinking, you pick up the cup and put it back into your car's cup holder – where it doesn't even belong in the first place! Of course, you should throw it away instead. But that cup has been there so long, it seems like it should be there. In other words, it's comfortable.

Negative Thoughts about Money

Without realizing it, you have done the same thing with negative thoughts about money. You'd be better off if you would stop believing that money doesn't like you, but like that Starbucks cup, it just seems like it should be there.

Some examples of negative thoughts about money include:

• People like me don't become financially successful

• Debt and financial trouble are part of life

• Money is hard to make

• I'm not good with money

• I don't deserve abundance, wealth or prosperity

• I shouldn't want financial success because that's greedy

• Only dishonest people have lots of money and I'm an honest person

• Money only leads to trouble

• Money isn't important, it doesn't lead to happiness and it won't solve my problems

• If I wait, things will get better

Do any of those statements strike a chord? If one of those sentences makes you think, "That sounds exactly like me," you're off to a good start!

The Tapping Recipe

"I see EFT as a method that stimulates the body's electrical meridian system enabling a release of stuck patterns of emotions, beliefs and behaviors." ~ Gary Craig, Founder of EFT

The Reminder Phrase

For each tapping session, you're going to choose a reminder phrase. In the previous scenario, you would select one of those phrases. For example: "I'm not good with money." This is a statement you believe to be true about yourself and your situation. The most important thing about the reminder phrase is that it brings on a negative emotion.

This may be a bit painful. But the truth is that we have to draw these negative feelings of fear, anxiety, anger or sadness out in order to dispel them.

The point of the reminder phrase is that it hits you right in the gut. When you say this phrase to yourself, it should give you an almost physical sensation of pain. As you continue your tapping sessions, you'll watch this pain gradually disappear. Once it's gone, you'll be free to achieve the financial success you're dreaming of.

The Set-Up Phrase

The set-up phrase is a positive affirmation that you'll repeat during the tapping session. The purpose of the set-up phrase is to identify your fear or pain for what it is – just fear or pain. You "put it in its place" by identifying it.

The second purpose of the set-up phrase is to accept that about yourself. Only when you accept these things can you begin to work on dispelling them.

The traditional phrase for tapping goes like this:

"Even though I have this _____, I deeply and completely love and accept myself."

Into the blank, you enter the target you want to tackle. This could be something like:

Limiting or negative belief about money

Fear of being financially stable/ successful

Problem about how I handle money

Procrastination problem

Low self-image about money

And so on ....

You can change up this format if you'd like, saying for example:

"I love and accept myself completely even though I have this problem handling money."

The important thing is that there are two elements – acknowledgement of the problem and accepting yourself. As long as these two elements are there, you can create any affirmation that works well for you. When you apply EFT to the root cause of the problem, the relief will be permanent.

Saying Is Believing

When you first start tapping and saying your affirmation, it'll be strange because you don't actually believe it. Limiting belief about money? Fear of making money? It sounds crazy because you don't have it at all – you WANT money. At least, your conscious mind does.

And that's the rub – you're not speaking to your conscious mind but to your subconscious mind. At first you won't believe the words that are coming out of your mouth, and that's the way it should be. Just say the words and they'll have their effect.

Tuning In

Once you have identified a target, tune in to the problem. What this means is that you should focus all of your attention on this problem. You must be fully present with it. This can be very easy or quite difficult, depending on how your conscious mind sees the problem.

If it's obvious that you have a fear of making money, it's easy for you to visualize this. Identifying your target and tuning into it is no problem. But if it's buried deep within your subconscious and your conscious mind rejects it, it can be difficult.

For example, let's say that after much reflection, you realize that you're afraid of financial stability. But your conscious mind still clings to the idea that you desperately want to be stable. In other words, it insists that there's no problem. Yet your subconscious realizes that strong money management practice means controlling spontaneous urges to spend money.

As long as that subconscious belief remains outside your conscious beliefs, you'll never achieve your goal of financial strength. Tapping helps to draw out these subconscious controlling beliefs.

When it's hard to tune into the problem, you may need some help. Try to recall the memory of an incident in the past when you had an "ah-ha" moment and realized this block was holding you back.

For example, you may remember a time when you were given a large sum of money, but that voice in the back of your mind said, "Well, this won't last long!" Or perhaps someone offered you the perfect job, but you never called back because of your deep hidden fear. Put together a collection of these memories to focus on when you're tuning in.

An Example

Here is an example. You identify your target – a limiting belief that you're not good with money. When you say to yourself, "I'm not good with money," you remember mistakes you made in the past and this triggers an almost physical feeling of pain and disappointment.

That is your reminder phrase – "I'm not good with money."

Now, your set-up phrase would be something like this: "Even though I have this limiting belief that I'm not good with money, I love and accept myself completely."

Now, you're ready to tap!

How to Tap

Tapping is the easy part. It takes only a few minutes to learn. Like all practices, you have to insert it into your daily habits.

When using EFT, we tap with the fingertips. You should tap firmly but lightly (there's no need to pound away!). Traditional tapping uses the index and middle finger of one hand only, but modern practitioners use both hands. The energy meridians on both sides of your body are the same. Most therapists recommend tapping alternately with the right and left hand on the same meridian points on either side of the body.

Before tapping, remove eyeglasses, headgear, ear buds, bracelets, watches and anything else that will get in the way.

The Tapping Points

EFT uses specific tapping points located throughout the body. These points have been identified by traditional acupressure as the confluence points of your body's energy flow. Like acupuncture and acupressure, tapping is a set of techniques which utilize the body's energy meridian points.

The meridian points are stimulated by tapping on them with your fingertips – literally tapping into your body's own energy and healing power. The meridian points are:

The Top of the Head – This point is at the crown of your head, right at the center of your skull.

Eyebrows – The eyebrow points are located where your eyebrows start on the inside of your eyes.

Sides of the Eyes – There are meridian points located just on the outside of your eyes. The meridian points are located between the temple and the rim of bone that juts out just before your eye starts.

Under the Eyes – A meridian point is located about an inch under each eye.

Under the Nose – There is one meridian point located between your nose and lip, right in the center of where you'd have a moustache. The spot is in the groove found there. You can tap here with one or two fingers alternating.

Chin – A meridian point is found in the groove between your lips and chin.

Collarbones – There is a meridian point located just below each collarbone. Put a fist to the base of your chest where you would knot a necktie. You'll feel the two collarbone knobs jutting out. The meridian points are just below the bone where it's soft and sensitive if you press.

Under the Arms – The under arm points are just below your armpit. If you're a woman, they're where your bra strap would be. They're approximately level with your nipples.

Wrists – The wrist points are about three finger widths up your hands from the creases of your wrists. You can tap these points with your fingers, whole hands, or by tapping both wrists together.

Karate Chop – The karate chop point is on the pinky side of your hand, so called because this is where you would hit something with a karate chop. Here you can tap with one, two or three fingers.

*On all of the facial points you can tap with one or two fingers of each hand. On most of the body points, you can use four fingers (two of each hand) and in some points more as indicated above.

This drawing on the next page will help you locate the tapping meridian points on your body and the side of your hand.

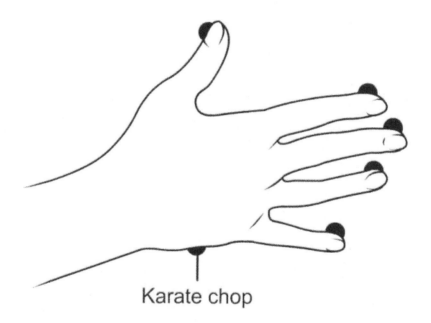

Karate chop

Tapping Points

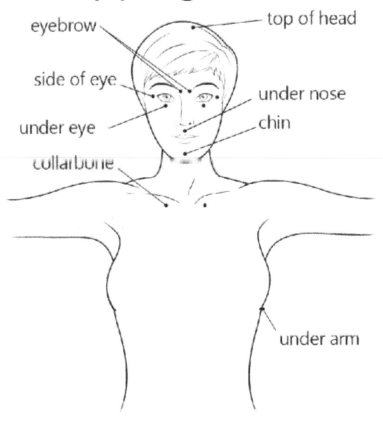

eyebrow

top of head

side of eye

under nose

under eye

chin

collarbone

under arm

At first, you may not get the points exactly. Beginners often use 2-3 fingers so as to tap a wider zone. It may also help to ask a therapist or experienced tapper to show you exactly where they are.

The Tapping Sequence

In acupuncture, each meridian point relates to a certain organ or function of the body and Chinese medicine has all of this meticulously mapped out. In EFT, we're doing something far less drastic and since there are only a few meridian points we use, we're not concerned with these relations. All the tapping points are useful for removing emotional blocks.

Tapping is done in a sequence. There are variations on this sequence but here is the standard way it's done:

Identify the target problem or issue you want to go after.

Rate the intensity of the emotion you feel from 0 to 10. This is done so that you can chart your progress. As you perform EFT, you'll gradually see the intensity of this emotion decrease. This means you're making progress. You'll also rate your feeling again at the end of each session to see if the sequence is working or if you need to change it. Bear in mind that many feelings have more than one scene and more than one aspect, meaning that each aspect must be cleared before you are done.

Choose a reminder phrase. This is a phrase that brings on the negative emotion you hope to dispel. In the case of finances, it may be something like, "My money problem," "Fear of being wealthy," "I can't save money," "I'll never be prosperous," etc.

Remember that the whole point is to focus on this pain or painful emotion. Sometimes the trauma from a memory is too upsetting to bring to mind. In this case, just use the words "that terrible thing that happened" or similar wording.

127

Start by tapping **the karate chop point** and repeating your reminder phrase. The reason we start with the karate chop point is that it's associated with psychological reversals, and that's what we're doing here – reversing a negative thought or belief about yourself. Say the set-up phrase three times while tapping five to seven times.

Start tapping through the meridian points. Start with the eyebrow point and work your way down your face and body, ending with your under arm points. When you start each new point, repeat the reminder phrase. This will bring the painful memory or feeling back to the surface where it needs to be tapped out. Again, tap each meridian seven to ten times, and then move on to the next. After the point under the arms, finish with the top of the head.

Repeat. Once you've worked your way through the whole sequence, start with the karate chop and go for another pass. Go through each of the meridian points in the exact same way a second time.

Reassess your feeling. Repeat the reminder phrase and again rate it on a scale of 0 to 10.

It's recommended to repeat these tapping sessions several times each day. It sounds like a lot, but one session takes only a matter of minutes. And remember, you can do it virtually anytime, anywhere.

Try performing your tapping session standing in front of a mirror. Looking at your reflection in the mirror helps to focus on the activity.

Reassessing Your Pain or Emotional Level

Some people experience immediate results, finding that they score a 0 for their pain or anxious feelings. If that's you, you're lucky. Great job!

For most of us, we only get partial relief. However, when you're really suffering, this relief helps. EFT provides short-term relief for stressful situations. If you just had a major meltdown, one tapping session can help you get back to a calm and balanced state, just like a quick meditation or creative visualization would.

For a long-term problem like changing your attitude toward personal finances, it's going to take longer. Reassessing your pain helps you to chart progress.

After one EFT session, your pain should be lower on the scale than it was when you started. Minor adjustments can help you bring that rating down lower and in the long run, make the pain disappear completely.

EFT Troubleshooting Guide

"Success is often achieved by those who don't know that failure is inevitable." ~ Coco Chanel

What if you reassess your pain and find that it's the same – or higher!? Surely this means that EFT doesn't work!

Actually, this is a good thing. It provides you valuable feedback. It tells you that something needs to be changed. There are many variables at play here, so let's look at what may be keeping you from removing your negative blocks.

Wrong Target

Much of EFT's success depends on the target. If you choose the wrong target, you won't get the results you expect from the technique. But how do you choose the right target?

Sometimes it takes some soul searching. We naturally hide from pain, so it can be difficult to pin down. But you'll know it when you find it – psychological pain at high levels produces physical symptoms. When you identify it, you'll feel it in your body. It could be anything from a queasy feeling in your stomach to a nervous twitch in your eye or a migraine.

You may have a discovery moment, one of those "AHAs" as you process through the tapping sequence. This realization may be the true issue that finally has surfaced.

Here's an example. Let's say that you identify your pain and you come up with this reminder phrase – "I'm not capable of saving money."

130

How does it make you feel to say that? If you feel nothing at all, you're not really getting at your deepest inner pain. Maybe what you've identified is just one symptom of a bigger underlying problem.

If you're not feeling it, try asking yourself "why?" After a bit of thought, you may realize that the reason you can't save is that you don't want to have money. Having money saved means you've got something to lose. Maybe you have a phobia of things being taken from you.

Now, try it out – "I'm afraid of losing something valuable." When you say it, it's undeniable. It hits you straight in the heart.

The subconscious isn't logical or rational. For this reason, you may choose a reminder image instead of a reminder phrase. Try to think of a memory that gives you a painful feeling.

To take the same example from above, maybe your pain is triggered by the memory of the day you lost your house because of debt. This is the underlying cause of your anxiety about losing something valuable. Instead of a reminder phrase, evoke this memory using words to describe it.

<u>Wrong Wording</u>

Your set-up phrase needs to be worded so that it's straight to the point and accurate. It needs to be truthful and it has to be about you, using "I" in the first person. It should be in your own words and it

131

should be in the first words that come to mind when you think about your problem. In other words, don't try to make it complicated or fancy.

If you need help, here's a free writing exercise therapists use. Think for a minute about your financial problems and then start writing. Don't think first, but let the words spew out. Write until you're tired of writing. If you've been truthful in your writing, there will be many phrases there that can be used.

Pick the phrase that identifies the problem best and plug it into this set-up phrase template:

"Even though _____, I deeply and profoundly love and accept myself."

Keep in mind that EFT often doesn't work when the problem is too general or global. It needs to be as clearly defined as possible, in as specific words as possible. It needs to relate directly to you. It could be that you haven't quite gotten it specific enough yet.

Trouble Accepting

Sometimes the difficult part is really meaning that you accept yourself. This is harder than most people realize to do. We naturally want to change things we don't like about ourselves. But for now, just let it go and accept. Tell yourself that it's alright to have these limiting beliefs and fears because you know you'll shed them.

The power of affirmations helps here. When you repeat a phrase, it sinks into your subconscious and has an affect there. You can try practicing your set-up phrase as an affirmation to help with this. Practice in front of a mirror and look straight into your eyes as you repeat it.

Here are some other things that might help. First, realize that no matter how many negative beliefs or thoughts you have, you're still doing much better than most people. At least you're taking steps to work things out.

Another thing to realize is that the basis of acceptance is love. It's the unconditional love a parent feels for their child. Love is an action, not a state of being. When you say this phrase, you've decided to love and accept yourself. You even love the limiting belief! Accepting is an action that you choose to do.

Too Much at Once

EFT works because you identify a problem, bring up its related energy disturbance, and then tap the meridian points to clear this disturbance. If you're trying to take on too many problems at once, you won't activate the energy disturbance clearly and tapping won't work.

Your set-up phrase may say something like "Even though I can't save money and I'm afraid of financial success..." These are legitimate problems that can be addressed with EFT, but not both at one time. You should address only one problem at once.

The above example is fairly obvious, but you may also be taking on two problems at once by accident. This happens when you're focusing on one problem but getting distracted by another. You may be focusing on a belief you have that you don't deserve abundance but your mind is being troubled by mounting debt problems.

When this happens, it may be worthwhile to shift your focus. Maybe the problem distracting you is where you should be putting your efforts. You may want to redefine your specific goals.

Wrong Meridian Points

When tapping doesn't work, it's much more likely to be for the above reasons than because you are missing the tapping points. Unlike acupuncture, where the points are clearly defined on the body, tapping uses approximate points. The reason is that you don't need to be exactly on top of the energy confluence. If you're close, the tapping will have the desired effect.

However, if a certain point in your sequence doesn't feel like it's releasing energy the way it should be, you might experiment with how you're tapping. As mentioned in the section about how to tap, some meridians can be tapped with two fingers or more, and there are variations on how some points can be tapped. You can try experimenting and see what works (or consult an EFT therapist for help).

Not Enough Repetition

Some people experience the benefits of EFT immediately. For most, it takes time. As you can see by just reading the tapping instructions earlier in this book, it's quite an involved process. One session involves a lot of tapping and affirmations!

But this is why tapping works. It's the constant repetition, both during a session and as sessions are repeated over the course of days and weeks that makes it work. Be patient and stick with the technique for a while. It usually takes a bit of persistence before you see results.

If your rating is not getting lower (or is getting higher) after days of tapping, you may consider working with an EFT practitioner.

Advanced Tapping Tips

"Dear old world", she murmured, "you are very lovely, and I am glad to be alive in you." ~ L.M. Montgomery, Anne of Green Gables

So far we've covered the basics of tapping. You have more than enough to get started. However, making small changes to your EFT routine can make a huge difference. Once you've started and feeling results, you can experiment with advanced EFT techniques to help you remove tough emotional blocks.

Gratefulness Tapping

EFT is all about removing the negative and replacing it with the positive. One of the best ways to crank up your positivity and keep it pumping all day long is to be grateful.

Gratefulness tapping works because as you tap and release your body's energy flow, you imbue it with positive feelings by focusing on things that are going well in your life. You're saying "thanks."

To do gratefulness tapping, follow the same routine as you would with your regular tapping. But instead of your set-up and reminder phrase, use a gratitude phrase.

Gratitude phrases usually start with, "I'm grateful for" or "I'm grateful that." Here are some examples:

I'm grateful for the food on the table.

I'm grateful that I own my own home.

I'm grateful for the support I get from friends and family.

I'm grateful that I've managed to save a little money.

I'm grateful that I'm making more at my job than I did last year.

I'm grateful for the financial wisdom my parents taught me.

I'm grateful that I've overcome a financial obstacle.

Gratefulness reinforces your positive feelings while banishing the negative. In fact, it's easy to take a negative and turn it into a gratefulness phrase. For example, let's say you haven't managed to save as much money as you'd like. Instead of focusing on your disappointment, turn it around and say, "I'm grateful that I've put away some money." It's a bit like the glass being half-full or half-empty.

And that's the key to being grateful. It's in how you see things. We all too often focus on what we want and don't have, rather than what we have. You can always stay positive about your finances when you focus on the things you have, like food on the table, a job, a home, healthy kids and pets. Spend a moment reflecting on things unrelated to your financial weaknesses. You'll come up with something to inspire gratitude.

"What If…" Statements

What-if statements are, as the name suggests, statements where you ask, "What if…?" Okay, technically they're questions, but we won't split hairs.

"What if" statements are great for EFT to remove financial blocks because they help get rid of limiting beliefs. When you ask "what if," you explore all the possibilities. This is the direct opposite of limiting yourself.

For example, if you suffer from the idea that you don't deserve abundance in your life, a good what it statement can free you of that. What if you truly did deserve it? As you say these words and visualize this new reality, it dispels the negative belief that limits you.

137

Some examples of what if statements are:

"What if I deserve financial success and abundance?"

"What if I inherited these negative ideas about money from someone else?"

"What if I'm releasing a mental block right now?"

"What if I can attract abundance and wealth if I just relax and accept myself?"

"What if I'm just as deserving as anybody else?"

Again, use these phrases as you tap. There's no need to use the full tapping structure of rating your feeling, using a set-up phrase, and so on. Just go through your sequence while repeating a "what if" statement.

Tapping Into Abundance

"Abundance is not something we acquire. It is something we tune into."

~ Wayne Dyer

As you tap and remove emotional blocks, you'll begin to see clearly how you've been limiting yourself. You're not wrong for doing that. We create limiting beliefs through the ideas we inherit from our parents or other influences, and from the misinterpretation of life experiences.

Think hard about your beliefs about money (note: here we are working with the beliefs the EFT way. This is still working on releasing foundational charges using money as the topic; as it is one of the most charged subjects). There's a good chance that you learned these things by not only listening to but also watching your parents. You saw how they handled money and it shaped your opinion.

Think about your financial history. Your limiting beliefs may come from life experiences that you misinterpreted. This is usually done by associating these experiences with "always" and "never," two words that are deadly for positive thinking.

For example, let's say that you lent money to someone and they never paid it back. You made a mistake and there's nothing wrong with that. In fact, mistakes are good because you can learn from them. But if you tell yourself, "I always make unwise money choices," you're creating a story about yourself that's not true. You did once or maybe several times, but that doesn't constitute "always."

When you go through the process of daily tapping, these revelations begin to come to you. It's like peeling back the layers of an onion only to find more layers to peel!

A new story about you emerges, and this story goes something like this…

You can do anything you'd like to do. You can make anything you want happen. You can create the financial situation, security and abundance in your life that you want – all you need to do is to let go of the charges and master programs. The first step you have already taken, which is to release the charges around money. This alone will make a huge difference in your life.

Now, before we move into the next step (Dreaming), I want to let you know that I have instructional videos and more tools offered that deals with money, the main charges and master programs in my online coaching program called 'The Limitless Program'. You can find more information about it here:

http://www.TheLimitlessProgram.com

Below is a bonus section with more tapping scripts to help you clear any money or abundance blocks. Enjoy.

BONUS SECTION TAPPING

EFT Tapping Script Samples

Disclaimer: For many emotional issues, the negative feeling you are having is caused by a disruption in one or more of your meridians. Any stimulus which reminds you of a past trauma recreates the disruption in the present and leads to the negative feeling. The combination of tapping the meridian points while holding the negative thought in mind neutralizes the disruption in your meridians and dissipating the negative feeling. Before tapping my recommendation is to get assistance of a trained NLPQ

Practitioner or consult with a mental health professional if you feel uncertain. Remember you are 100% responsible for your results. The disclaimer in the beginning of this book is valid here and applies to all the contents of this book.

Creating an EFT Tapping script is very personal. In this document you will find 3 different scripts each addressing a different issue/problem/specific event/belief/emotion. The process goes through different stages, but the verbiage varies. As you become more comfortable with the tapping process, you will create your own scripts that work for you. These are examples to get you started practicing tapping.

If you want to get more hands-on experience and master tapping you may want to explore a more formal training as an NLPQ Practitioner.

You can start that journey here: http://www.NLPUniversity.co.uk

Tapping Script Template

1.   State the problem

Choose an issue/problem/specific event/belief/emotion that you would like to release or transform. Pay attention to where in your body you feel this intensity. eg in the stomach, shoulders, hands, temple etc., when you think about your issue/problem/specific event/belief/emotion.

2.   How does this make you feel? Rate the level of intensity: Low 0 to High 10

On a scale of 0-10, rate the intensity of the issue/problem/specific event/belief/emotion with 10 being the greatest distress/intensity and 0 being no distress/intensity at all.

3.   Perform the Setup Statement while tapping the Karate Chop point 3 times

The set up statement is a description of your issue/problem/specific event/belief/emotion followed by an affirmation or choice statement.

Choose either the affirmation or choice method and say the set up statement 3 times out loud while tapping the Karate Chop point on the side of your palm with 2-4 fingertips. Some people like to do this step while looking into a mirror.

4.   Round 1 Tapping Points

Tap each of the meridian points 5-7 times while saying the Reminder Phrase, e.g. "fear of having money."

5.   Round 2 Tapping Points

Once you finish processing through all the tapping points in Round 1, repeat. This time you can replace the Reminder Phrase with other phrases that come to mind or feelings you are feeling. For example, the Reminder Phrase "fear of having money" may become "feeling incapable of managing money."

6.   Round 3 Tapping Points

Process through each of the 8 Meridian Points again. Continue to change up the Reminder Phrase as you process through the points and new feelings or thoughts come to mind.

7.   Take a deep breath

Stop. Take in a deep breath and release it slowly.

8.   Rate the intensity (0-10)

Rate the level of intensity again. Is it the same as it was when you began? Less? More?

If the level of emotion/pain/belief/problem intensity is above a 2, repeat the entire sequence with slight modifications to the reminder phrases.

Instead of "fear of having money" the phrase is "this remaining feeling of fear of having money."

The goal is to eventually get to a "0" level where the feeling is nothing. This may take several sessions. However, some people "get to zero" in their first session. In either case, you can't go wrong tapping. After the first day of tapping, reflect on the process and how you felt. You can repeat the exercise more than once a day. It is important to insert a tapping routine into your daily schedule. Once you accomplish a release from an emotional barrier, move on to a new one.

How to Tap Quick Reference

Tap with the tips of your fingers. Some people use the first two fingers, other use four finger tips (see pictures for tapping points earlier in this chapter).

The Karate Chop (KC) is done by tapping the side of one hand at the Karate Chop acupressure point with the tips of four fingers on your other hand.

You will process through the nine meridian points tapping with two or four fingertips. The short code for each point is below:

Eyebrow (EB)

Side of the Eye (SE)

Under the eye (UE)

Under the nose (UN)

Chin (CH) this is a point between your chin and your lower lip.

Collarbone (CB)

Under the Arm(UA)

Top of Head (TH)

EFT Tapping Script Example: Tapping Away Fear of Having Money

Sequence #	Step	Example
1.	State the problem	"I have this fear of money/wealth/financial strength."
2.	How does this make you	9

	feel? Rate the level of intensity: Low 0 to High 10	
3.	Perform the Setup Statement while tapping the Karate Chop point 3 times.	Even though I have "this fear of wealth," I **deeply and completely accept** myself
	The traditional tapping Setup Statement uses an affirmation such as I **deeply and completely accept** myself.	or
		Choice: Even though I have "this fear of wealth," I **choose** to feel the strength financial wealth brings.
	Another tapping model uses the "choice" mechanism.	
		Repeat two more times… "Even though I have this fear of wealth, I deeply and completely accept myself"
		"Even though I have this fear of wealth, I deeply and completely accept myself"
4.	Round 1 Tapping Points	(EB) – say "this fear of wealth"
		(SE) say "this fear of wealth"

		(UE) say "this fear of wealth"
		(UN) say "this fear of wealth" (CH) say "this fear of wealth"
		(CB) say "this fear of wealth"
		(UA) say "this fear of wealth"
		(TH) say "this fear of wealth"
5.	Round 2 Tapping Points	(EB) – say "I know money brings security"
		(SE) - say "Maybe it's the responsibility"
		(UE) say "Perhaps the fear is my friends will use me"
		(UN) say "or fear of additional responsibilities"
		(CH) say "this fear of wealth"
		(CB) say "this fear of responsibility"
		(UA) say "this fear of responsibility"
		(TH) say "this fear of wealth"

6.	Round 3 Tapping Points	(EB) – say "this fear of wealth" (SE) - say "what if I am wealthy" (UE) say "I can have someone help manage the money"
		(UN) say "this fear of wealth"
		(CH) say "the responsibility doesn't have to be mine"
		(CB) say "this fear of wealth"
		(UA) say "this fear of being responsible with money"
		(TH) say "I can control money decisions"
7.	Stop. Take in a deep breath and release it slowly	Pheeeeewwwwwwwwww!
8.	Rate the intensity (0-10)	2

In this case the rate of intensity after the exercise is a 2. Process through the script again, but in Step #3 change the Setup Statement to be: "Even though I have this remaining fear of wealth, I deeply and completely accept myself."

147

EFT Tapping Script Example: On finding your true passion in life

Sequence #	Step	Example
1.	State the problem	"I have this anxiety about not knowing my true passion in life"
2.	How does this make you feel? Rate the level of intensity: Low 0 to High 10	9
3.	Perform the Setup Statement while tapping the Karate Chop point 3 times. The traditional tapping Setup Statement uses an affirmation such as I **deeply and completely accept** myself. Another tapping model uses the "choice" mechanism.	Even though I have this anxiety about not knowing my true passion in life I **deeply and completely accept** myself. or Choice: Even though I have this anxiety about not knowing my true passion in life I **choose** to allow the answer to become clearer every day.

		Repeat two more times…
		Even though I have this anxiety about not knowing my true passion in life I **deeply and completely accept** myself.
		Even though I have this anxiety about not knowing my true passion in life I **deeply and completely accept** myself.
4.	Round 1 Tapping Points	(EB) – say "this anxiety about not knowing my true passion in life"
		(SE) say "this anxiety about not knowing my true passion in life"
		(UE) say "this anxiety about not knowing my true passion in life"
		(UN) say "this anxiety about not knowing my true passion in life"

149

		(CH) say "this anxiety about not knowing my true passion in life" (CB) say "this anxiety about not knowing my true passion in life" (UA) say "this anxiety about not knowing my true passion in life" (TH) say "this anxiety about not knowing my true passion in life"
5.	Round 2 Tapping Points	EB: "I want to know – but I'm really blocked" SE: "I don't know what my true passions are!" UE: "How can I not know this?" UN: "How frustrating!" CH: "I'm so indecisive!" CB: "I can't take a stand – but it just isn't clear to me yet" UA: "I don't know what to focus on" TH: "I don't know what activities will bring me the

		most joy in life"
6.	Round 3 Tapping Points	Moving Into the Positive:
		EB: "But maybe I do!"
		SE: "Perhaps there's at least a glimmer..."
		UE: "I choose to be completely open to these clues"
		UN: "And tune in to the wisdom of my intuition and Highest Self"
		CH: "This wise part of me which knows all of my true passions"
		CB: "And will reveal them to me in due time"
		UA: "I look forward to a life of passion and purpose"
		TH: "Every day I'm more tuned in to all the guidance I need to know my true passions in life!"
		***
		Tapping in the Positive –

		Tap all 8 points with this statement: "My true passions become clearer and clearer to me all the time."
7.	Stop. Take in a deep breath and release it slowly	Pheeeeewwwwwwwwww!
8.	Rate the intensity (0-10)	1

EFT Tapping Script Example: Don't Deserve to Have Wealth or to Receive Money

Sequence #	Step	Example
1.	State the problem	"I have this anxiety about not knowing my true passion in life"
2.	How does this make you feel? Rate the level of intensity:	9

	Low 0 to High 10	
3.	Perform the Setup Statement while tapping the Karate Chop point 3 times.

The traditional tapping Setup Statement uses an affirmation such as I **deeply and completely accept** myself.

Another tapping model uses the "choice" mechanism. | Even though I feel undeserving of making money with what I love to do, I completely love and accept myself without judgment.

Even though making money with my passion just doesn't feel right, it feels greedy and wrong, and I am struggling with that, I love and accept myself anyways.

Even though it isn't really true that I accept myself, it is so hard to accept being poor while I do all this great work in the world, I choose to allow myself to get ready for a shift.

q |
| | | |
| 4. | Round 1 Tapping Points | (EB) – say "I don't deserve to make money doing what I love"

(SE) say "I don't deserve to make money doing what I |

		love"
		(UE) say "I don't deserve to make money doing what I love"
		(UN say "I don't deserve to make money doing what I love"
		(CH) say "I don't deserve to make money doing what I love"
		(CD) say "I don't deserve to make money doing what I love"
		(UA) say "I don't deserve to make money doing what I love"
		(TH) say "I don't deserve to make money doing what I love"
5.	Round 2 Tapping Points	EB: "is it right?"
		SE: "to get paid for having fun"
		UE: "I don't feel I deserve it"
		UN: "How frustrating!"
		CH: "I feel guilty!"
		CB: "I don't feel that I

154

		deserve to get paid"
		UA: "Making money should be hard"
		TH: "is it right to make money so easily?"
6.	Round 3 Tapping Points	Moving Into the Positive:
		EB: "What if this is the way it is supposed to work!"
		SE: "I wish I didn't have to feel this way"
		UE: "I don't ask others if they deserve their pay"
		UN: "I wonder why I was so lucky?"
		CH: "Do I want someone to take this away?"
		CB: "What else would I do if I didn't do this work?"
		UA: "I wonder if it is really true that I don't deserve"
		TH: "What would happen to the people I serve if I stopped serving them?"
		***

		Tapping in the Positive – Tap all 8 points with this statement: "I am grateful that I have the courage to help others doing something I love to do."
7.	Stop. Take in a deep breath and release it slowly	Pheeeeewwwwwwwwwww!
8.	Rate the intensity (0-10)	1

Chapter 6: DREAM (Step Four)

What Do YOU WANT?

How to Design a plan for your life

From the time you were small, you've had thoughts, ideas, and dreams about what you wanted to be when you grew up. You most likely imagined the type of home you wanted to live in and where in the world you wanted to put down roots. You might have daydreamed about the career you'd have and the friends you'd hang out with.

As you matured, your innermost goals for your future morphed several times over the years.

Now, here you are, all grown up and living your life. You probably have a job and may be in a serious relationship. But at this moment, are you living a life that you'd choose to be living? Does your life fit you? Is your life going as you'd planned? Or did you even have a plan?

As you read this chapter, reflect on how you're living currently and ask yourself, "Is this what I want for my life?" As you examine your life, you'll be encouraged to thoroughly think through specific elements of your existence you might like to change.

The purpose of this chapter is to help you develop a life plan that will lead you to the life you desire.

How Do You Feel About The Major Aspects Of Your Life?

To get started, get a notebook to record ideas and thoughts that will form a new or revised plan for your life. Label it as your Life Plan notebook.

Next, spend some time thinking about these aspects of your life: Home, career, love relationship, family, friends, health, character traits, hobbies, and intellectual/cultural pursuits.

What does your ideal life look like?

Although no one's life is perfect all the time, a reasonable goal is to feel satisfaction, joy, and a sense of comfort and well-being in your own life in most of the above aspects of your existence. Let's take a look at each area.

"If you don't design your own life plan, chances are you'll fall into someone else's plan. And guess what they have planned for you? Not much."
—Jim Rohn

Your Home

One of the most important aspects of your life is your physical living environment. It includes the location where you live (city and state), the type of home in which you live, and the physical furnishings and arrangement within your home. Where/how you live profoundly affects your everyday life.

Is everything about your home just the way you'd like it to be?

Location of Your Home

Do you live in the location you would select to live in right now? If your answer is 'yes,' then you're in good shape. However, if your answer is 'no,' where would you like to live? What would it mean to move there? What is holding you back from moving to the location you desire?

160

Are you limited to living in a certain place because of your work? Most importantly, what steps would you need to take in order to relocate to the city/state of your choice?

At the top of a page in your Life Plan notebook, write "Desired Location." Write your target location on the left side of the page. On the right, list all the steps you need to follow to move to your target location.

Consider these sample steps for your Life Plan:

1.   Brainstorm cities to live in. Narrow choices to 2 cities.

2.   Research the cities on the internet. Make plans to visit the cities within the next 6 months.

3.   Check into the possibility of getting a job transfer. Determine whether there's an opportunity to request a job transfer to the city of choice. Ask staff at work about this issue.

Type of Residence

Do you live in an apartment and wish you lived in a house so you could have your own yard to garden and take care of? Or is it the opposite — you'd like not to be tethered to the constant work of maintaining your yard year-round.

Are you living in the type of home (apartment, house, or condo) you want to live in? Write down all your hopes and dreams about the type of home that attracts you. For example, if you now live in a house but would rather live in a condo to enjoy a more carefree lifestyle, make note of it.

Include in your Life Plan your specific goals about the type of home you prefer. Then list the steps you'll take to accomplish what you want.

Possible steps for your Life Plan:

1.   Call a realtor to discuss the worth of the house. Determine if it's feasible to sell now.

2.   Look for condo residences within 30 minutes' radius of work. Take a look at a few units.

3.   Evaluate budget to determine whether moving at this time is workable.

Furnishings and Room Arrangements

As you spend much of your life in your own home, it's important that it be comfortable and suitable for everything you want to do while you're there. If you love color, paint the rooms the shades you love. If you've got interests in great art, hang reproductions of your favorite artists' works in every room.

As you write this section of your Life Plan, think about how you can surround yourself with things you love and have furniture you like that also fits your needs.

If someone who knows you well were to tour your home, would he see the influences in it as truly representative of you? Does your home accurately reflect who you are just the way you'd like it to?

Record in your notebook what you'd like to change about the set-up of each room of wherever you live. Maybe you'd like to do away with the formal dining room and make it a game room or relaxing place to read or paint instead.

Here are some examples of steps you might write:

1.   Paint living room. Buy some light taupe-colored paint.

2.   Find sleeker-looking furniture for living room. Check consignment shops for a gray or black modern-looking sectional sofa and large glass coffee table to hold books and magazines.

3.   Measure bookshelves in bedroom to see if they'll fit in the living room after painting.

Where you live, the type of home you live in, and the furnishings are some of the most integral aspects of your everyday life. To live your best life, your home ought to reflect your overall personality and make you happy. Does your home setting fit these requirements?

If not, write down what you desire in these areas. Be specific. Keep in mind you're in the process of designing the life you seek. You deserve to be happy.

"Everything's in the mind. That's where it all starts. Knowing what you want is the first step toward getting it."

–Mae West

Career and Work

Since your career encompasses about a quarter of your life if you work full-time, you hopefully love what you're doing and have great passion for it. Work is your bread and butter — you support yourself and your family with the work you do. Your career is the very basis of your financial life and brings stability and necessary routine to your life.

Let's ponder that very thing — your job. Is the career you're working in now the type of work you'd opt for? Do you enjoy what you do? Or can you at least say you're glad to have your job and believe it serves as a stepping stone to a grander career for you in the

164

future? Are you where you want to be career-wise? Why or why not? What can you do to get there?

<u>This aspect of your Life Plan might include steps that look like these:</u>

1.   Ask supervisor about pursuing more training in accounting.

2.   Check local community college for a class on writing small business plans.

3.   Post resume at CareerBuilder.com to begin looking for another job.

Regarding your work, what changes could you make to feel more passion and excitement about your work?

Plan a realistic course of action to follow regarding your career that will make you happier and arouse your interest and creativity. Be honest with yourself about your career as you design this segment of your Life Plan.

"A good battle plan that you act on today is better than a perfect one tomorrow."
–General George S. Patton

Love Relationships and Family

Partner relationships and having a family are probably at the top of your list when it comes to what you want in life. Having a deep, enduring love life can improve your health and even increase your life span.

Finding a cherished life partner and having a family are probably either on your list or else you're already blessed with the entities of love and family.

It's important to occasionally re-evaluate these life aspects in order to experience long-term the joys and fulfillment of having close, satisfying relationships.

Love Relationships

Finding and solidifying a love relationship might be one of your main goals in life. How is your love life going? Are you pleased with the partner you've selected and the way the two of you spend time together? Is there anything you want to work on to enhance your love relationship? Or do you see it as just about perfect?

Perhaps you haven't yet found that special someone. Are there choices you can make regarding how you spend your time that would make it more likely you'd encounter someone with similar interests as yours? Make a note about any plans you have for your love relationship.

Love relationships are integral parts of a fulfilling life. Ensure you ponder your love life and address it in your Life Plan.

Give your love relationship the attention it truly deserves by considering whether it truly meets your wants and needs. If there are things you want to change about your special relationship, include those goals in your Life Plan.

<u>You might write steps such as:</u>

1. Talk with Sue about spending more time together, like having a date every Saturday evening.

2. Discuss my concerns about John's developing pattern of coming home late for dinner. Figure out a workable solution to the issue.

3. Join the golf league at the Country Club to meet other people who also like to golf.

Family

Getting married, having and raising children, and fostering enduring family ties might likely be important elements of your life. A family provides a supportive, loving network like no other. When all seems lost, turning to your family to spend special time together can lift your spirits more than anything or anyone else.

Do you want a family? Or do you already have a family and have a goal to spend more time with your loved ones? How does your family fit in to the plan you have for your life and future? Ponder these issues. If it's something you're interested in, include family in your plan.

Possible steps:

1.   Agree to work only one Saturday a month to have the other Saturdays to spend with family.

2.   Talk with Jane about wishes to have a baby soon.

3.   Ask Cousin Jim to meet for coffee one Sunday morning a month.

Your close connections with others make up some of the most fulfilling parts of your life. Therefore, address your wants related to your love relationship and family in your Life Plan. It will help you crystallize what you're seeking from these cherished relationships.

"If you love the life you live, you will live a life of love."
—Unknown

Friends

When you're designing a Life Plan, it's feasible that you'd include friendships. After all, the more supportive of a network you have the more satisfied and content with your life you'll be. To live your best life, you'll want to have wonderful friends.

Engaging with friends on a regular basis enriches your life in so many ways. During time spent with friends, you engage in fascinating conversation and enjoy your favorite activities with people you care about. Do you have friends? Did you meet your friends during various situations in life, such as high school, college, work, and your neighborhood?

Do you find your friends interesting? Are they helpful when you need it? Do you return the favor occasionally? Reflect on your friends. Do you hang out with the type of friends that you want in your life? Do you have no friends at all? Maybe you believe you have no time for friends.

<u>Your Life Plan steps regarding friends could look something like:</u>

1.　　Attend the neighborhood block party in May. Try to make friends with at least 2 people living nearby.

2.　　Make friends with people who attend the Business Morning Club on Tuesdays. Plan to get to know better at least 3 people from the club.

3.　　Go out with co-workers at least 1 Friday night a month.

Write in your notebook what you want to have in the way of friends. If you want 2 or 3 more good friends, write it down. What is your ideal plan for friendships in your life? If you're completely satisfied with the array of friends you have and the amount of time you spend with them, mention in your Life Plan that all's well related to friendships.

"The world steps aside for those who know where they are going."
–Anonymous

Health

Your physical condition is one of the most salient aspects of a plan for a good life. Your ability to manage your feelings and release your negative emotions is paramount to living a peaceful and satisfied existence.

Physical Health

Are you in the best physical shape you can be? If so, how do you do it? It might be wise to include your blueprint for good health in your Life Plan.

If you'd like to make some changes regarding your health, what changes would you make? What can you do to improve your physical self?

Are you willing to make the physical changes you desire? Do you want to do it? Decide if there's anything you want to have in your plan related to your physical health.

If so, go into detail about what you want and will do. For example, state you want to engage in regular exercise for 30 minutes a day 5 days a week. If you want to reduce your cholesterol and blood pressure readings, include such goals with specifics in your notebook.

As mentioned in prior sections of this book, designing the health section of your Life Plan requires you to be quite specific about what it is you want and the steps required for you to accomplish your goals. The more specific your plan, the more likely it is you'll follow it to live the life you desire.

Items like these could be included in the physical health portion of your Life Plan:

1. Get off blood pressure medicine. Go on the DASH Diet to lose 18 pounds. Walk 20 minutes a day 6 days a week.

2. Have a yearly medical examination every January.

Emotional Health

Your emotional health plays a role in everything you do. How you react when there's a challenge at work or when your partner disagrees with you is a result of your emotional health. Your overall moods spring from your emotional health.

Using EFT (you learnt in the previous chapter) and the other releasing techniques shared in 'The Limitless Program' online coaching program will help you release all 'negatives' and enjoy great emotional health. Make sure to include this practice into your Life Plan.

172

Do you feel satisfied and content most of the time? Is it customary for you to exhibit angry outbursts at others? Maybe you spend moments practically daily thinking about something upsetting that took place in your life a long time ago.

Examine your own emotional health. How are you doing? Take into account your emotional health when designing the health aspect of your Life Plan. Record what you want to do about any challenging feelings in your notebook.

<u>Steps in the emotional health section of your Life Plan could be:</u>

1.   Release on a daily basis.
2.   Use EFT on people and events that is draining my energy.

Your physical and emotional health's are two aspects of life that permeate all other areas of your existence. If you're in the best shape you can be physically and emotionally, good for you. However, if you desire to make some adjustments in these areas of your Life Plan, write down exactly what you wish to do to achieve what you desire.

"Let our advance worrying become advance thinking and planning."

–Sir Winston Churchill

Character

Elements of your character also figure in to the big picture of your life. Perhaps you believe you already possess the character traits you deem important. However, it's worth your time to consider this very relevant area of your life.

Possessing and displaying strong character is necessary to live a life you can be proud of. Do you have the character traits you believe to be important or that you admire? Do you strive to show the patience your grandfather always demonstrated that you so appreciated? Have you developed your mother's strong work ethic you were always so proud of?

Now is the time to inventory your own character traits. Maybe you've got the traits you've aspired to but have a few you'd like to alter or improve on.

Under the "Character" heading in your notebook, write down whether to keep doing what you're doing or how you want to alter some of your personal qualities.

<u>Be specific in your Life Plan – for example, you might write:</u>

1.   I will listen better to co-workers and make efforts to understand them better so I can be a mentor and help others.

2.   Read a book about patience. A goal is to increase patience.

3.   Work harder by finishing all projects I start within two weeks. Keep listing of my projects and check them off as I complete them. Seek supervisor's guidance to improve my work habits.

Having positive character strengths will lead you toward a fulfilling life. In your Life Plan, you'll want to address character traits specifically.

Consider what's important to you regarding your character and then document your goals and the steps you'll take to achieve them in your Life Plan.

"Make no little plans; they have no magic to stir men's blood.
Make big plans, aim high in hope and work."
–Daniel Burnham

Hobbies and Activities

Mental health experts have long known the incredible impact that chosen hobbies and activities have on a person's life. Do you have hobbies you adore?

Collecting baseball cards or old dishes might bring you the greatest emotional lift ever. Being involved in the local Chess Club or volunteering at the library could be the icing on your cake of life.

Take a look at these sample Life Plan steps:

1.   Sign up for golf lessons next month. Learn how to play golf. Practice golf once a week in addition to lesson time.

2.   Call the community theatre and inquire about try-outs for their next production.

Whatever your beloved hobbies and activities, ensure you've included them in your Life Plan. What changes would you like to make in this realm of your life? Are there hobbies you're tired of doing? Would you like to develop an interest in a new activity? Write down the activities you've always wanted to do in your spare time.

Realizing the impact of your hobbies and activities on your life is important to your levels of contentment and satisfaction. Consider hobbies and activities as important parts of your Life Plan.

"Great minds have purposes; others have wishes."
—*Washington Irving*

Intellectual and Cultural Pursuits

Having intellectual and cultural pursuits in life may or may not be important to you.

If thinking great thoughts, engaging in stimulating conversation, and being in a constant state of learning are things you love to do, then it would make sense for you to include something about intellectual pursuits in your Life Plan.

Learning a second language, reading all of Shakespeare's works, or attending plays and cultural shows are relevant pastimes if you want to be involved in cultural activities. Consider what some of your secret passions might be. For example, have you always wanted to re-read some of the classics you read in high school so you can truly enjoy and understand them?

Perhaps your ethnic background and country are subjects you've always dreamed of exploring in depth. Can you imagine more fascinating pursuits than these? You deserve to take the time to engage in whatever cultural pursuits that draw your interest.

Check out these possible items in this category of your Life Plan:

1. Attend one play every 3 months. Call about special pricing at the theatre.

2. Research my cultural heritage. Join Genealogy.com to construct my family tree.

3. Check out travel DVD at public library on Spain.

Are you happy with the level of these pursuits you currently enjoy? Outline specifically how you'll pursue them in your Life Plan.

"Planning is about bringing the future into the present so that you can do something about it now."
—Alan Lakein

Summary

Creating your Life Plan is a fluid process because life itself is ever-changing. Situations transform, people grow, and unexpected events occur. So re-evaluating your Life Plan from time to time is the smart thing to do.

Your Life Plan will ensure you live wherever you wish in the way you want. Your plan will provide a pathway for you to do work you're passionate about and cultivate relationships with partners, have children and family, and fraternize with friends you adore.

A plan will even help you set up your spare time so you're spending it doing hobbies and activities that bring you satisfaction, fascination, and joy.

Make your physical and emotional health a focus of your Life Plan — the healthier you are the better life you'll live. Re-visiting your Life Plan from time to time will allow you the opportunity to continue to work to strengthen your character and possess the qualities you deem important.

Finally, reviewing your Life Plan will show you whether you're pursuing activities that expand your intellect and taste for cultural events.

Also, use EFT on any negative emotions or doubts that might come creeping up as you write and pursue your Life Plan.

If you strive to truly embrace life at its fullest, make your own plan and then take every step from this day forward to make it happen! Live the life you truly want by discovering the value of having a Life Plan.

"If you want your life to be a magnificent story, then begin by realizing that you are the author and every day you have the opportunity to write a new page."

–Mark Houlahan

Chapter 7: DECIDE (Step Five)

Discovering Your Life Purpose

"Resolve to be thyself; and know that he who finds himself, loses his misery." Matthew Arnold

What is a Life Purpose?

"The purpose of life is a life of purpose." **Robert Byrne**

When you hear the term "life purpose," you probably envision people who are following a higher calling, like priests, nuns, missionaries, doctors and scientists. In other words, people who are doing important work in the world.

People like this are certainly living a purpose, but you may be surprised to learn that a life purpose doesn't have to be so magnanimous either. In fact, throughout the pages of this e-book, I'm going to demonstrate that purposeful living can take virtually limitless forms – most of which you've probably never considered before.

The dictionary defines purpose as:

1) an object or result aimed at : INTENTION

2) RESOLUTION, DETERMINATION

What does this tell us? A "purpose" can be as simple as an intention or a resolution. So, a "life purpose" is really nothing more than a commitment or resolve to live in a certain way and achieve specific objectives. If that sounds a bit confusing, don't worry. We're going to clear it up in a hurry.

For now, just know that you DON'T have to have a deep inner "calling" in order to have a life purpose. You don't have to give away your worldly possessions and become a missionary in order to make a positive difference in the world.

In fact, you may be surprised to discover that realizing and living your life purpose will be a comfortable and enjoyable process. Bit by bit, you'll create life circumstances that are totally suited to who you are, your likes and dislikes, natural talents, and much more.

It's the kind of inner journey that changes everything – from emptiness to satisfaction, from boredom to passion, from aimlessness to unbridled joy and beyond!

Do you have trouble believing that's possible for you? Do you see your current circumstances as brick walls that you can't break through? Do you worry that you're stuck forever exactly where you are?

If so, I ask you to set aside any feelings of doubt and skepticism for now. Be willing to believe that your life DOES have meaning, and be open to the insights that are about to follow.

Where Does a Life Purpose Come From?

One of the reasons people often doubt that they have a life purpose is because they've been led to believe that a life purpose is akin to those "spiritual callings" mentioned earlier. If they don't feel an inner calling, they decide that there probably isn't a specific purpose for their life – or worse, that their life has no meaning at all.

If you ask enough people, you'll probably find that there are two basic schools of thought regarding life purpose:

1)   Those who believe that a life purpose is something we are born with, that it is planted into our souls before we are born and we MUST achieve it. It's our destiny, so to speak, and we have no choice in the matter.

2)   Those who believe that fate and destiny don't exist and we have the power (or "free will") to choose our life purpose and do anything we want with our lives.

Which group do you belong to? Fate and destiny, or free will? There are no right or wrong answers to this question; only what you feel in your heart is the right answer for you.

If you're still not sure, I'd like to propose a workable compromise for you. What if a life purpose is something you are born with, but you also have full control over how and when you achieve it? What

184

if, with a little introspection and planning, you could move naturally and easily toward your life purpose without feeling like you "have" to do specific things?

Personally, I do believe that each of us has a pre-destined life purpose – BUT it is something that comes very naturally to us. It's not something that's difficult, unpleasant or burdensome. A life purpose, in my opinion, is realized by getting to know your authentic self, exploring your natural talents and interests, and choosing the best possible medium to share them with the world.

We'll be covering those concepts further shortly, but first, take a moment to decide how you feel about your own life. Do you believe you have a purpose, or that you can choose one?

How Do You Know If You Have a Life Purpose?

When it comes to life purpose, people usually find themselves in one of three places:

1)   They don't worry about whether they have an official purpose or not; they simply live their lives doing the things they feel drawn to.

2)   They know exactly what their purpose is, and they joyfully work at it each day.

3)   They believe they have a purpose but have no idea what it may be or how to find out.

Which group do you fall into? Members of the first group probably would not be reading this book, and members of the second group would probably be too busy living their purpose to read about it.

The majority of people who read this book probably fall into group #3. If you're not sure if you do, consider the questions below:

• Have you ever felt like you were supposed to be doing more with your life?

• Have you ever yearned to use your natural talents to contribute to the world?

• Have you ever felt like your current or previous jobs didn't use your talents fully?

• Do you ever feel like you are wasting time on things that aren't important to you?

• Do you desire to serve others in a bigger way but don't know how?

• Has your daily routine become predictable and boring?

• Do you ever wonder if "this is it"?

• Do you yearn for greater meaning in your work and other activities?

If you answered yes to most of those questions, you're probably ready to discover greater meaning and purpose in your own life – whether you see it as awakening a pre-destined purpose or choosing one you want.

Life Purpose vs. Living Purposefully

"It is never too late to be what you might have been." George Eliot

There are many people who feel intimidated by or resistant to the concept of a life calling. Maybe you do too. Do you worry that having a life purpose means surrendering to a higher power and giving up control of how you spend your time? Do you worry that your life purpose will end up being something unpleasant or taxing? What if your life purpose turns out to be draining or boring? What if it demands more than you are willing or able to give in time, energy and commitment?

These types of fears are completely groundless. If you could poll everyone on the planet who believes they are living their true life purpose, I bet they would all say the same thing: "I'm so HAPPY!"

Everyone who dares to live their life purpose describes it along the lines of "coming home" or "doing what I was born to do." They do what matters most to them, they enjoy it fully, and it fits perfectly with the rest of their lives.

That's not to say that a few sacrifices won't be necessary at times, but I think you'll find that they are not overly painful or difficult. In fact, they may be downright freeing once you let go of your fear and doubt.

Please don't worry that living your purpose means you have to give up control of your life. You are always in control of your own life, purpose or no purpose!

In fact, I want to encourage you to adopt a new outlook for your life – that of "living with purpose" rather than "having a purpose".

Living purposefully means CHOOSING your purpose. Choosing how you spend your time. Choosing how you will use your natural talents to create more joy and meaning for yourself and others.

Even if you believe that your life purpose is pre-destined, this new outlook can still work for you because you'll automatically choose the path that has already been laid out before you.

Do You Really Need a Purpose?

If you are one of those people mentioned earlier who doesn't worry about having a life purpose, you may wonder what all the fuss is about. Is a life purpose even necessary?

Some people would say that everyone has a purpose whether they know it or not. But is it a bad thing to be unaware of a higher calling in life? What if you feel content with your life as it is right now? Do you have to conceive some lofty purpose in order to feel content and make a positive difference in the world?

No. You don't need to have a specific purpose in life – unless you feel like something is missing. If you are content with your life as it is, you are doing something right. Either you're already living your purpose or you simply don't feel the need for one. And there's not a thing wrong with that.

However, since you are reading this book it is possible that you are seeking something – even if you wouldn't classify it as an actual "calling". Maybe you simply crave more passion, meaning, fun, direction or any number of other qualities. And a life purpose (or living purposefully) can definitely provide those things and more.

Benefits of Living Purposefully

In fact, you may be surprised to discover just how rewarding a purposeful life can be!

Here are just a few of the benefits:

• Greater focus in your daily activities – rather than feeling adrift.

• Increased discipline when it comes to productivity and achievement.

• Passion and motivation! When was the last time you felt excited about your day?

• Personal empowerment – being in control of your own life.

• Meaning and fulfillment. Knowing that your life (and everything you do) matters.

• Energy and vitality! Purposeful living energizes your mind, body and spirit.

• Peace and contentment. Knowing you are exactly where you need to be.

I could go on and on, but these are probably the most notable benefits of living purposefully. If you've never felt strengthened, empowered or fulfilled by your activities before, you have definitely not discovered your purpose yet (or chosen one that resonates with you). Once you do, every moment of your life takes on greater meaning and passion – rather than seeming pointless and boring.

How Do You Find Your Purpose?

"Learn what you are, and be such." Pindar

It's Already Within You!

"Finding" your purpose is a misleading concept because it's not something you have to go out and "get," but rather something you need to turn within and claim. You've already got it – even if you haven't consciously realized or chosen it yet. Of course, whether you believe it is already within you or not, you still need to "find" it in some sense. How do you do that? By looking in the most obvious places – your passions and interests.

Your purpose will always be something that:

• You feel passionate about

• You are naturally good at

• You already love to do

• Is important to you

Remember earlier I mentioned that your fears about your life purpose being unpleasant are groundless? It's absolutely true. Why would you be given a life purpose that doesn't match the essence of who you are?

Would the universe expect a musical prodigy to spend his life crunching numbers in an accounting firm? Would the universe expect you to wait tables when your true passion is childhood education? How would these situations serve anyone? They wouldn't!

Your life purpose will ALWAYS utilize your greatest passions, talents and interests. No exceptions. Does that inspire a little sigh of relief for you? It should.

<u>Identifying Your Passions</u>

Before you can discover your true life purpose, you need to uncover the clues that lead to it. Namely, things you are good at, feel passionate about, love to do, and are important to you. Take a look at the worksheets on the next few pages and start filling in a few ideas for each of them. You don't have to completely fill them. In fact, you're looking for the most obvious answers here - even there are only a handful of them in each category. Focus on things that have been a major part of your life or occupied your thoughts a lot - and it's okay to have the same answers on multiple sheets.

Topics or Subjects I'm Passionate About

These would be topics or subjects you feel passionate about, like personal growth, education, arts and crafts, music, pets, spiritual development, business, poetry etc. Anything you think about and enjoy quite often.

Activities I Love To Do

These would be tangible activities like sports, working out, painting, singing, writing, reading, cooking and so on.

193

Things I Am Naturally Good At

On this sheet, list all of your best talents, skills and experience. Focus on actual activities that you do easily and well, either because you're naturally good at them or because you have a lot of experience with them.

Things That Are Important to Me

World events, situations, groups, causes, people, animals and more that are important to you. Focus on things that impact the world in general, not just things that pertain to your own life, your own family, etc.

Putting the Pieces Together

Now that you've identified some of your strongest passions and interests, look again at the worksheets. Do you see any connections or patterns between the items you listed? You may not yet have a full picture but more like a handful of puzzle pieces - you see that they could fit together but you're not sure how.

Here's a good way to make the big picture clearer:

Imagine that you are preparing to take a journey. What do you need? First, you need to establish a clear destination. You need a map that shows you how to get to your destination. You need a method of transportation to travel there; and of course, all modes of transportation require fuel to power them.

Your life purpose is very much like a journey.

• The things you love to do are the vehicle you travel in.

• Your natural talents are the map that shows you how to get to your destination.

• The things that are important to you ARE the destination.

• Your passion is the FUEL that powers the whole operation.

<u>With every purpose, you need:</u>

1)   A passion for it. (Your passions)

2)   A commitment to it. (Important to you)

3)   A tangible way to share it with the world. (Activities you love to do)

4)   The ability to do it well. (Your natural talents)

When these things come together, you've got a virtual explosion of passion, meaning, fulfillment, empowerment – and purpose!

Do you see now why it's important to get clear on the four worksheet categories? Every item you write on those lists offers a possibility and each of those possibilities contain still more possibilities!

Of course, you won't be following all of them right away, but more likely choosing one to start with. You can always incorporate others later if you want to. For now, I strongly encourage you to start with the ONE that speaks most powerfully to you, the one that makes you feel excited and joyful.

Let's use an example to show how this all comes together:

Things I Love To Do	I'm Passionate About	I'm Naturally Good At	Things of Importance
Cooking	Health	Giving advice and encouraging people	Children
Working out	Fitness	Writing	Women's issues
Writing	Alternative healing	Problem solving	Domestic violence solutions
Teaching	Helping people	Blogging and web design	Environment preservation

This is just a partial collection, but you can see at a glance that there are obvious connections between the items here. Perhaps your lists won't have such obvious connections, but the more you study them they'll start to jump out at you.

What kind of life purpose could this person choose? Here are just a few possibilities:

- Writing and publishing books on health and fitness
- Empowering women through conscious living
- Publishing a children's health and fitness magazine
- Establishing a "Mommy and Me" fitness/educational center
- Speaking in schools about fitness for children
- Writing cookbooks with healthful recipes
- Becoming a licensed dietician
- Becoming a personal trainer

There are truly endless possibilities here. In fact, every item on the list above could be narrowed down even further. For example, this

197

person could become a personal trainer specializing in children's fitness, and combine that with speaking engagements and demonstrations at schools, churches and other community events. He or she could also expand later by writing and selling cookbooks geared toward existing clients. Do you see how many directions this could go?

Your own lists are also ripe with limitless possibilities – you just need to narrow down the best choice for you. How do you know which is the best choice for you? You'll feel your creative juices start to flow! Your heart rate will speed up, your mind will start racing with neat ideas and you'll feel excitement bubbling up from within you. When that happens, you are on the right track!

But . . . what if you still don't know what your purpose is? What if your worksheets are blank and you have no idea what to write on them?

I Still Don't Know What My Purpose Is!

"Knowing others is wisdom, knowing yourself is enlightenment." Lao-Tzu

Most people will have some solid ideas about their passions, interests and talents – but not everyone will. If you found yourself struggling to come up with items to write on the worksheets, take comfort in the knowledge that you're probably not alone!

Maybe you've spent your life doing what was expected of you and you never had the freedom to explore your passions before. Maybe you are so saddled with responsibilities that even now you can't find time to do the things you love – even if you knew what they were!

The good news is that it's not going to be difficult to find out. And once you get that ball rolling, your only challenge is going to be choosing between the many choices you have available. To discover your passions, talents, interests and important issues, try one or more of the suggestions that follow.

Think Back to a More Magical Time

Children naturally gravitate toward things they enjoy, have you ever noticed that? If you have children of your own, each of them probably has very different personalities, likes and dislikes. This uniqueness is obvious even when observing children that aren't your own.

The question is: what did you like and dislike when you were a child? What types of television shows did you watch? What toys were your favorites? What costumes did you favor for holidays and special events? Who did you dream of being when you grew up?

All of these memories hold clues to your authentic self. Even though your actual activities have changed since childhood, it's likely that you still gravitate toward the same preferences.

Make a list of your favorite memories, the ones that bring back a warm glow of happiness or pleasure. Then look closely at them and try to identify their core essence. Why did they make you feel so happy? Can any of that essence be brought into your current circumstances?

Windows to Other Worlds

Another great way to find clues about yourself is to visit the bookshelves in your home. Books have often been described as windows looking into other worlds, but they can also be windows looking into you!

What types of books are in your home? Do you prefer fiction or non-fiction? What topics are most of your books about? Which books have you read over and over again until they are well-loved and dog-eared? These quiet companions will tell you a lot about your interests and passions.

If you're not a big reader or don't have any books of your own, take a trip to your local library. Walk around and look at the shelves of books. Which categories make you want to stop and browse some more? Take notes on the types and subjects of books that seem to capture your attention most. You can also use this same technique with magazines, music CDs, and videos/DVDs you have around your home.

World Wide Possibilities

The world wide web is also a fantastic storehouse of clues about your passions! Take a trip through your Favorites folder. What types of websites do you visit frequently? Do you belong to any forums or groups?

You can also visit large, general-interest websites and browse their topics. Click on things that catch your attention and keep a running list so you can explore the topics further later on.

Social Clues

Also be sure to take a closer look at your social life. What do you like to do with friends? What types of activities do you enjoy, with friends and by yourself? Most of us do have a social life, even if it is limited to a few outings a year!

If that doesn't yield any clues, try making a list of activities you always WISH you had time to explore. Have you always been fascinated by photography? Do you feel a twinge of longing when you walk through an art museum? Do you have a hard time tearing your gaze away from a gorgeous garden?

Keep a running list of activities and subjects you feel even the slightest interest in, and little by little they may blossom into full-blown passions!

How to Live Your Purpose

"Simply give others a bit of yourself; a thoughtful act, a helpful idea, a word of appreciation, a lift over a rough spot, a sense of understanding, a timely suggestion. You take something out of your mind, garnished in kindness out of your heart, and put it into the other fellow's mind and heart." Charles H. Burr

Once you've awakened to the many possibilities that exist for your life purpose, you might feel a bit overwhelmed by it all. So many choices! So many great ideas and not enough time to put them all into action! How do you know which one is the right one? Or are all of them equally right?

There is no easy answer to that question except to say that you'll know it in your heart. The best choice for you will just "feel right." You'll be thrilled by the idea of doing it and you'll be eager to get moving right away!

Again, remember that you don't have to take on all of the possibilities right away. There's nothing wrong with starting on one small aspect and then gradually branching out. In fact, I strongly encourage you to do that.

As exciting as it is to discover a new purpose for your life, you may still have fears and doubts you'll have to work through, as well as physical actions that need to be taken in order to make it all come together. That will take time in most cases.

Work at your own pace and don't try to rush the process of transformation. Remember that for every outer transformation you make, you'll also be making some inner transformations!

This is especially true if your current life circumstances have moved you far away from your true life purpose.

Whether due to external influences or inner fears, you may have created a life that doesn't even come close to including your true passions and interests.

In fact, that's much more common than you might think!

Sometimes we don't know what we want to do with our lives, so we allow others to direct us. Perhaps your parents or your high school guidance counselor chose your current career. Maybe you followed friends and modeled your activities and goals after theirs because you didn't know what else to do.

No matter your unique situation, it's possible to change it all – one step at a time. First, let's talk about career and life purpose.

Does Your Purpose Have to Be Your Career?

Did you notice that our example chart was geared toward a life purpose that is also a career? Many people do choose to turn their life purpose into a career, but you don't have to. Maybe you already have a job that pays well and you enjoy it, but you also feel a need for something more. Maybe you are retired or financially independent and don't want a job or business but you want to serve others in meaningful ways.

The form your purpose takes is completely up to you, whether you turn it into a paying career or use it as a vehicle to serve others freely.

The Steps that Lead to Fulfillment of Your Purpose

Once you're clear on the form you want it to take, you'll need to begin planning and preparing for action. This is where many people stall. They know what they want to do, but putting it all together seems like a monumental task.

Living your purpose is no different than achieving any other kind of goal. You need a detailed PLAN to put it into action. With most goals, there are clear steps that lead to the final outcome.

Using the same example from earlier, let's look at some possible steps that would be needed to put this life purpose into motion:

• Receive training and certification for dietician/personal training

• Write the book(s) that will be published

• Decide on a location (will it be done from a home office, leased space, etc.)

• Create a website, blog or newsletter

• Learn marketing and promotion

• Network with others in the industry

• Secure financing for business start up

Depending on the form this person chooses for his or her purpose, there will be specific tasks that need to be completed before the desired outcome can take place.

The same will apply to your own purpose. You don't have to complete everything at once – you simply take one step at a time and move each puzzle piece into place. Gradually, the whole picture becomes visible and before you know it, you are living your purpose.

Take a few moments right now to list the logical steps you'll need to take in order to move forward on your own purpose. Include things like education and training, skills and experience you'll need to have, lifestyle changes, external help, resources or financing you'll need, and so on. If possible, try to list these things in chronological order, starting with the things that need to be done first before you can move on to the next items.

Steps to Be Taken

Once you've got some clear steps outlined, it's a simple matter of taking them one by one! When you do that, you keep moving forward and everything falls into place.

Do you feel doubtful about that? In fact, right now are you besieged with thoughts like this: "Who am I kidding? I don't think I can do this. I love the idea, but it's just not realistic. My job is so demanding and I don't have the money needed to start a business, not to mention the time investment needed . . ." – Stop right there. There's something important you need to know.

Your Purpose Isn't Just About YOU

"If I can stop one heart from breaking, I shall not live in vain." Emily Dickinson

It's Your Gift to the World

Before you allow your mind to run amok with excuses, fears, doubts and the like, I want to stress that this isn't about you. Yes, living purposefully is a fantastic way to get more meaning and satisfaction from your life. Most people start seeking a life purpose just for that reason. They feel empty and aimless, sick of living a life that doesn't fulfill them. There's nothing wrong with that, even if it may seem a bit self-serving at first glance.

But an interesting thing happens when people discover their life purpose and begin living it: they realize that their greatest joy and satisfaction comes from serving others. Their focus begins to shift away from what they might receive and moves steadily toward what they can share.

When you start seeing your life purpose as a GIFT you can give to others, you'll find that much of your fear, doubt and hesitation will fade away. You'll stop worrying whether you have what it takes to live your purpose and focus more on doing the best job you can do, simply because it's important to the people you're serving.

There's Something Special About You

Furthermore, it's important to realize that as grand and intimidating as your life purpose may seem from where you're standing now, you already have what it takes to achieve it.

When it comes right down to it, you ARE your life purpose. Your purpose is a perfect blend of the best parts of you: your passion, your talent, your interests, and the things that are very important to you.

You are meant to share these parts of yourself – this ESSENCE of yourself – with the world.

No one else on the planet has what you can offer. No one else will create the things that you can create. No one else has the power to touch people's lives exactly like you can.

Everything you touch, everything you do, everything you create is infused with your unique essence.

People Need What You Have to Offer

Not only is everything about you unique and special, but right now even as you read these words, there is a person (or more likely a large collection of people) who desperately need what you have to offer.

Do you have trouble believing that? Is it hard for you to imagine having something that others really need and want?

This is a common blockage because most people tend to see themselves as "average." Nothing special, just an average Joe or Jane.

If you take away nothing else from this book, I want you to know how limiting – and even destructive – such a mind-set is. You are one-of-a-kind, and seeing yourself as anything less will detract from what you have to offer.

Seeing yourself as special and unique is not vain. The point isn't to believe that you are better than anyone else – just different and equally as valuable.

And here's where it gets even better. By awakening to your own brilliance and power and sharing them with the world, you will be encouraging other people to do the same. In fact, you've probably already experienced that from the other end of the spectrum.

Have you ever seen someone doing something really well and felt an inner stirring? For example, perhaps you were feeling down and you heard a song on the radio that seemed to rekindle your inner fire, encourage and inspire you? Even better, have you ever seen someone doing something and thought to yourself, "I could do that! I've got a natural talent just like that, why aren't I using it?"

These people are living their own purpose(s), but at the same time, they are serving as living examples that will awaken you to YOUR purpose. Those experiences are not accidents. Whenever you feel a strong resonance with something or someone you see, hear or read – it's there for a reason.

Pay very close attention to that inner resonance because it holds clues to your own talents, passions, abilities – and ultimately, your life purpose. And once you begin living your purpose and sharing it with the world, you will be providing the same kind of wake-up call for others who resonate with you.

It's Not All Up to You

"Learn to do thy part and leave the rest to Heaven." John Henry Cardinal Newman

Just like your purpose doesn't affect you alone, you probably won't be fulfilling it all on your own either. As mentioned earlier,

210

you may feel a tad overwhelmed or intimidated by what you've discovered is your life purpose.

Your mind may be swirling with thoughts like these: "How on earth will I be able to do this myself? What if I can't do it? What if I screw it up and let everyone down? What if I can't secure financing? What if I can't find the resources I need to make this happen?"

These worries are completely normal, but also unnecessary. Here's why: the bigger and more powerful your life purpose is, the more help you'll receive to achieve it.

There are two ways to look at this:

1)   If you believe that your life purpose is pre-destined, then you also have to believe that the universe (or your choice of governing divinity) would not give you an important purpose and abandon you without a clue about how to complete it.

2)   If you believe that you choose your own purpose, then you also have to believe that you have the resourcefulness, ingenuity and smarts to make it happen.

Both scenarios mean one thing: that you are not undertaking this journey without tools or guidance! Either you already have what you need to complete your life purpose, or it will come into your life at the exact moment you need it. That might include meeting other people who have a similar or related purpose and want to team up with you, or it could mean having the perfect opportunities appear right when you need them most!

In fact, there is a little thing called "synchronicity" that will surprise you again and again once you begin following your true purpose. If you are standing at the threshold of something new and exciting and you're terrified that you can't do it all on your own – get ready to be awed and amazed!

Everything you need to complete your purpose will appear right when you need it – or you'll at least know how to get it, if it doesn't come directly to you. Your job in the meantime is to set aside your fears and doubts, and simply begin moving forward. Take one step, then another. The rest will all fall into place beautifully.

Possible Challenges You'll Face

"Conquering any difficulty always gives one a secret joy, for it means pushing back a boundary-line and adding to one's liberty." Henri Frederic Amiel

That last paragraph may have intensified a sense of doubt in your mind. Is it REALLY true that "the rest will fall into place beautifully" if you just keep moving forward?

Yes - and sometimes no. It's important to understand that you may face a few challenges while you're working toward your life purpose. Sometimes these challenges will come from inside your own mind (negative thoughts, doubts, and the like which you now can use the EFT process to eliminate), and sometimes they might be external obstacles you didn't expect to encounter.

This section is going to cover some of the most likely challenges you may face, and give you tools and strategies for overcoming them beyond releasing them with EFT.

Fear of Change

This is a common challenge for people who are firmly entrenched in their current life circumstances. If you're in your forties, fifties or older, you may think it's too late to conceive a new life purpose now.

Perhaps you've already spent years building a stable career and you don't want to "rock the boat" now because you stand to lose so much.

Even if you're younger but have a lot of responsibilities or demands on your time, it may seem monumentally difficult to change directions now without creating a whole lot of havoc in your life.

No matter your specific situation, it's never too late to make changes that will contribute greater value to the world and create greater meaning and fulfillment in your own life.

213

Of course, you don't have to make a giant leap from one lifestyle to another, either. Start small if bigger changes overwhelm you. Spending even an hour a day on meaningful activities can create greater satisfaction that will seep into other areas of your life too.

Maybe later you'll decide to not only "rock the boat," but jump out of it entirely and swim to another shore! Or maybe not.

The only thing you have to consider is what you want and what you're willing to do to have it. Small changes or big changes, it's completely up to you.

EFT is also a perfect process to release on any fears that might come up. You just follow The Tapping Recipe you learnt earlier in this book.

Lack of Belief

As mentioned previously, you may not really believe that there is anything special about you. You may not believe that you have the ability to create a meaningful life. Maybe you still don't believe that you have a purpose or can choose one, even after reading this book.

Whatever lack of belief you may have right now, it's okay. Understand that inner conviction usually comes from doing, not necessarily from trying to convince yourself.

If you have completed the worksheets on the things that are important to you, you are passionate about, interested in and naturally good at; you've already got a sense of the right direction to move in.

If you also took the time to identify some clear steps that will move you toward what you want, there is nothing left to do but start taking those steps!

As you do, you'll begin to believe little by little. With every success, every challenge you stare down, every obstacle you overcome, you'll begin to believe in yourself and the importance of what you're doing. Eventually, momentum will take over and the process will become a lot easier.

If You Do What You Love, Will the Money Follow?

This challenge applies to you especially if you intend to turn your life purpose into a career. One of the biggest obstacles people in this situation face is uncertainty about how to transition from their current career to a new one that relates to their life purpose.

For example, you might have a stable job with a reliable income right now, but don't have the financial freedom to quit and do something that may or may not be financially lucrative.

The concept of "do what you love and the money will follow" is often touted by self-development experts, but is it realistic? I love to sit on my behind and watch movies - but I can't see that bringing in a paycheck any time soon!

Unfortunately, it's usually not as simple as "doing what you love" and then watching the money roll in.

However, there is a grain of wisdom in this concept, with one notable difference: if you can find a way to serve others while doing something you love, you can make money from it at the same time.

If you really want to turn your life purpose into a paying career, you need to find a way to monetize your passions. Depending on your personal situation, this may be something you can do right away and quit your existing job, or it might be something you'll have to build up to gradually. It will be different for everyone, so take some time to determine what will work best for you.

Charging Money for Your "Gifts"

While we're on the subject of money, there is another challenge that may create conflict within you, and that is the question of ethics when considering whether to charge money for your contributions to the world.

Many people believe that gifts and talents (usually referred to as "God-given") should be shared freely with others and never exchanged for monetary gain. While I can appreciate this charitable attitude, I really have to disagree.

Modern day society is driven by money, whether we like it or not. As lofty as it would be to donate all of your time and attention to others for free, you are really limiting yourself if you do that, which means you are limiting the amount of people you can help.

If you don't charge money for your talents and services, you will have to earn an income some other way unless you happen to be financially independent. In most cases, that means you'll have less time and energy to devote to your true purpose.

Personally, I see nothing wrong with charging money for gifts and talents, whether they are those of a plumber, doctor, artist, spiritual advisor or anyone else. If you are providing something of value to others, you deserve to be compensated for that contribution unless you choose to offer it for free.

Not everyone will agree with this, of course. Don't be surprised if you encounter a few stray "freebie seekers" with an over-inflated sense of entitlement, but don't let them worry you either. If you are truly providing something of value, something that really helps people, you are justified in expecting to be paid for your time, energy and expertise.

That doesn't mean you should focus heavily on the money, either. If you approach your life purpose with an attitude of "What's in it for me?" you could set yourself up for problems.

What kind of problems, you ask? For one, focusing only on what you stand to gain from your activities reduces the intensity of passion and joy you'll put into your purpose. You'll be so busy watching for the monetary returns that you won't be giving from a heart full of generosity and love.

Another problem that could arise is that you will gage your success by the amount of money you bring in, rather than the number of lives you are able to touch. In fact, you'll probably notice that the financial rewards grow naturally in proportion with the growth of your purpose. The more people you help, the more easily the money will come.

Finally, doing anything "just for the money" usually reduces your enjoyment of it. You can enjoy financial rewards, of course, but keep in mind that there are much more satisfying rewards to be had if you open to them

Overall, your main objective should be to serve – while also being open to the natural flow of abundance that comes along with success.

Of course, if you have no desire to earn an income from your purpose then this situation wouldn't apply to you; you would simply work at it as time and energy allows and call it good. There is nothing wrong with this approach either; it just depends on what your objective is.

Slow Progress

As you begin moving toward your life purpose, you may feel like you are moving through molasses. Maybe you'll bump into plenty of obstacles that will slow your progress, money might trickle in when you desperately need a waterfall, or you might simply seem to be moving at a snail's pace for no apparent reason.

When this happens, it's very easy to convince yourself that you must have been crazy to try living your purpose. If it was meant to be, wouldn't it be easier?

Don't do that to yourself!

First, understand that you are likely undergoing some major changes both within and without. There may also be external influences affecting your progress, and you have no control over those influences. Maybe it's a collection of factors, some of which you aren't even aware of.

No matter what is happening, do your best to make the journey itself the reward. In other words, don't get hung up on expecting a specific outcome in a certain timeframe. As long as you are taking the steps that you know will lead to your chosen destination, you are on the right track.

Instead, make it your mission to feel good about what you're doing right now. Trust that everything will work out exactly as it's meant to and focus only on doing your part.

When you do that, you avoid wasting time and energy on fear, doubt and frustration. You stop worrying about the end result and enjoy each step between here and there.

Balance and Responsibility

As great as it is to feel purposeful and passionate about your activities, it's also possible to become obsessive and take on too much, too soon. In fact, this likelihood increases the bigger your purpose is.

As much as we'd all love to change the world by 9:00am tomorrow, it may take a little bit longer.

When you first conceive your life purpose, you may find yourself wanting to hurry up and make it all happen overnight. Whether there are many people who need what you can provide or you feel desperate to change your own life circumstances, remember to take it slow. Keep balance with the rest of your life. Make time for proper self-care, rest and recreation. You won't be serving anyone if you end up burned out and exhausted.

On the flip side of this same coin is the importance of responsibility. Once you have realized your life purpose, you may need to do some substantial shifting around of your activities to make room for your new priority. And it IS a priority. It has to be.

If you don't make this new objective very important, you'll easily find reasons not to work on it. You'll complain that your kids are too demanding, your job is too stressful, you're too tired, you don't have enough time to yourself, and so on. And you'll go on feeling dissatisfied and unfulfilled for years, or even your entire lifetime.

In your own mind you'll have plenty of valid excuses for why you haven't achieved the dreams in your heart, but deep inside you'll know that you never fully committed to it and made it a high priority.

Finding a balance between these two extremes may not be easy at times, but with self-awareness and planning you can make the transition much easier for yourself.

Keeping Those Fires Burning

Self-motivation can be a tricky thing, no matter how passionate you are about your activities. Sometimes without realizing it you may find your attention waning or outer distractions interfering, which can throw you off track in a hurry.

You may find it helpful to come up with a mission statement to keep you on track. It can be a simple statement like, "My purpose is to educate and empower women in living healthier, more balanced lives," or it might be more detailed, such as, "I commit myself to writing, speaking and educating others on the subject of living purposefully. Every waking moment of my life will serve as an opportunity to inspire and awaken those who seek to be awakened."

Whatever kind of mission statement you choose, make it something meaningful to YOU. Something that will fuel your inner passion and keep you focused on your ultimate objectives.

Success in Dealing With Challenges

There are other possible challenges that could arise; it's impossible to cover all of them in these few pages. But no matter what kind of challenges you may face on your journey toward greater purpose and meaning, know that your attitude is going to make the biggest difference in the magnitude of the obstacles you encounter.

If you see them as daunting, overwhelming and immovable, guess what? You'll give up. On the other hand, if you choose to see them as temporary challenges that CAN be overcome, you'll do what it takes to get past them.

Rather than seeing these obstacles as threats, learn to see them as opportunities. Opportunities to strengthen yourself from within; opportunities to stretch your limits; opportunities to grow and develop as a person, and more. Challenges can be your best friends if you're willing to learn from them.

Surrendering to the Journey

"Today I know that I cannot control the ocean tides. I can only go with the flow . . . When I struggle and try to organize the Atlantic to my specifications, I sink. If I flail and thrash and growl and grumble, I go under. But if I let go and float, I am borne aloft." Marie Stilkind

As mentioned before, each of us has the freedom to choose what we do with our lives, but there is also certain wisdom in learning how to surrender to the journey.

Through sheer force of will you can achieve much, but at what cost? Learning how to surrender rather than forcing things to go your way can not only make things much easier, it can also create outcomes that are far better than you alone would have created.

Have you ever wanted something so badly that you made it your sole mission in life to get it? Maybe you had to work extremely hard or keep hammering away at obstacles until finally, victory was yours! And then what? Probably you experienced a bit of letdown or fatigue, disappointment that what you thought you wanted wasn't so great after all.

That's because so much of what we think we want actually comes from our ego-selves, the false self. The ego is the spoiled, petulant child within each of us. The part of us that cares only about our own happiness, our own comfort, our own gain. When we set goals and objectives from this state of mind, inevitably we are disappointed by them later because they serve only our immediate whims and desires.

Letting Your Inner Wisdom Lead

There is a wiser and more patient part of us, however. This part of us could be called our spirit, higher self, inner wisdom, or many other names. When we set our ego aside and allow this part of ourselves to take charge, everything suddenly becomes much easier.

Not only are we able to choose more lasting and satisfying objectives, we are also led to the simplest and quickest ways to achieve them. Struggle evaporates. Fear dissolves. Impatience is transformed into confidence and trust. When you surrender to this higher part of yourself, the entire journey becomes smoother, more magical, and more deeply satisfying.

It won't always be easy to set your personal preferences aside. Sometimes you'll find yourself getting hooked on doing things a certain way, or seeing a specific outcome from your efforts.

Self-awareness can help keep you more balanced in this respect, because you'll more easily notice when you're clinging, pushing or forcing circumstances, or resisting an easier way – even if you wouldn't have chosen it as "your way."

Choosing the Easy Way

Remember that for every objective there is an easy way and a hard way of accomplishing it. When it comes to your life purpose, your inner wisdom will lead you to the easy way, every time.

That doesn't mean effort won't be required. In fact, you'll probably work more diligently on your passions than you've ever worked on anything before! But it won't SEEM like work. It will seem fun and easy – even blissful.

Surrendering to the journey has another benefit too; helping you to keep your expectations in check. Rather than pinning all of your expectations on some distant outcome, you'll be better able to enjoy what you're doing now. You'll make the journey itself your objective. That doesn't mean that amazing outcomes won't result from your journey – quite the opposite!

The more attention and energy you put into NOW, the more powerful LATER will be. But you won't have to focus so hard on it to make it happen. You'll just naturally create it from one moment to the next.

Allowing Your Purpose to Evolve

Believe it or not, your life purpose will continue to evolve for the rest of your life, just as you will personally, spiritually, professionally – in all areas of your life, really. That's why it's not so important to have a nitty-gritty detailed idea of what your purpose is, but rather to look at the pieces that comprise it and begin taking action on them.

As you learn, grow and develop throughout your lifetime, so will your purpose. In fact, don't be surprised if you're doing something completely unrelated to the activities on your worksheets twenty years from now. Those initial insights may prove to be mere stepping stones that lead to something much bigger and better. Or they might end up being all you want to do, forever. It can go either way.

That's another reason why it's so important to let your inner wisdom lead. By doing so you'll stay aware of inner changes that might be moving you in another direction than you initially intended to go.

226

Living Moment to Moment

More than anything else, I want you to understand that living your life purpose isn't about trying to become someone you are not, doing things you don't enjoy or taking on all of the worthy causes in the world.

It's about coming back to yourself – your authentic self – and awakening to the potential that already exists within you.

Many of us, for most of our lives have gotten used to "playing small." We've been told over and over again that it's wrong to honor our uniqueness – let alone celebrate it.

We've spent a lot of time trying to blend in, be like everyone else and hide that glimmer of brilliance that wants to burst forth from us.

But doing so not only stunts our own growth, it deprives the world of something magnificent.

Through the exercises in this book you may have conceived a clearer idea of the specific activities that comprise your life purpose, or you may still be trying to figure it out – but understand that your purpose goes far beyond the things you do day to day.

When you believe that your life has meaning and make it your purpose to infuse that meaning into everything you do, you make every moment and every activity meaningful. Consequently, you are able to live with purpose no matter what you do, no matter where you go, and no matter how you and your purpose evolve over time.

You'll simply turn your entire life into a vehicle for positive change, growth, healing, awareness or anything else you decide to adopt as your mission.

Can you imagine a more powerful purpose than that? I sure can't.

May you enjoy ever-increasing passion, power and purpose in everything you do!

Congratulations! You made it. You have taken all five steps and if you followed all the instructions and exercises you will have noticed a dramatic shift in your life. Well done.

This might seem like the end but it's just the beginning. Your real journey begins now. Do it well. Enjoy the moments. More than anything remember that you are the hero in your life. Now live life like the hero you are.

To give you even more golden nuggets on your journey I have included a bonus chapter. This next chapter is called 'The Wisdom From The Heroes Journey'. Enjoy!

Chapter 8: The Wisdom From The Heroes Journey

The Wisdom From The Heroes Journey:

9 Life Lessons From Joseph Campbell

"We're not on our journey to save the world

but to save ourselves.

But in doing that you save the world.

The influence of a vital person vitalizes."

~ Joseph Campbell

Introduction

One of the most incredibly gifted philosophers of the twentieth century is Joseph Campbell. Campbell spent his life studying Native Americans and people of primitive cultures. His career culminated in teaching college literature and writing various books of critical acclaim. Much of Campbell's writing centered on finding meaning in our lives.

This guide shares some of his most well-known quotes and provides a discussion of what Campbell may have meant. Then, we'll provide quick action tips for each quote to tell you how you can apply the saying to attain the life you're meant to live.

You have the power to enrich your existence, and taking heed of Campbell's sage words will help you find it. Enlighten yourself in ways you may not have ever thought about.

Discover the life that only you can live through Joseph Campbell's wisdom.

1. "The Privilege Of A Lifetime Is Being Who You Are."

This rather heady quotation encourages you to examine the true meaning of the word "privilege." A privilege is a special benefit that others may not be privy to. In life, you have likely earned or been given your own share of privileges.

Examining the concept of privileges as it applies to you, consider some of the privileges you have. You may have been born into certain privileges, like being a member of a wealthy family or being born to parents who live in a beautiful seaside place, fascinating country setting, or bustling urban city.

You probably earned some privileges, too, like driving privileges when you were 16 to 18 years of age and voting privileges because you obey the laws of the land. And if you really think about it, you're likely enjoying many privileges right now.

In this quotation, Campbell seems to be saying that the single best privilege you can have, what he calls, "the privilege of a lifetime," is the ability to be yourself. In essence, he's asserting that the most wonderful benefit you'll ever possess in your life is being yourself, the person you're meant to be.

Apply these quick tips to make the most of this Joseph Campbell quote:

1. Ask yourself, "Who am I and who do I want to be?" Exploring these feelings that you have "deep-down" is relevant to the rest of your life. What kind of person are you now? Into what kind of person do you wish to evolve?

2. Describe the roles you live. It may sound a little silly, but get out some paper and a pen. Then list all the roles you have in life.

   * Your list will likely include things like, mother, father, brother, sister, friend, volunteer, salesman, business owner, sports nut, runner, artist, jewelry maker, golfer, and whatever other roles are important in your life.

3. Ponder whether or not you're comfortable with each role. Perhaps you spend a lot of time as a secretary, but you don't experience much joy with the work. Reflect on your level of comfort taking part in your various roles.

4. Spend some time thinking about what roles you'd like to add to your list. Without limiting your thoughts and ideas, quickly jot down what roles you'd like to be living, but aren't. Are you surprised and a little excited about what you came up with?

5. Make some of your desired roles happen. Now that you know who you really want to be, set out to make it so. Strive to be your own person.

   ✴ Focus on expressing your own wants and interests through the life you live.

   ✴ Decide to be whoever you want to be rather than just doing things as your parents wanted you to do or that you thought you were "supposed" to do.

Recognize that the best thing about life is the chance to be whoever you are or want to be. Reach out and grab that opportunity each day.

2. "Follow Your Bliss And The Universe Will Open Doors Where There Were Only Walls."

Campbell's famous "follow your bliss" saying is often quoted and occasionally misattributed to others. When you think of the word, "bliss," what do you think of?

According to the Wordbook Dictionary, bliss is a "state of extreme happiness." So, when you're following your bliss, you're going after whatever makes you happy.

The second part of the quote - about the universe opening its doors - could mean that life truly opens up for you when you're involved with things that bring you joy.

When you're engaged in pursuits that you love to do, you'll take more notice of your choices and be more willing to put your selected options into action.

If you think about a recent time when you were truly fascinated about something, you'll see what Campbell was referring to in this quote.

Let's say you became interested in weight-lifting. You started going to the health club and learning more about it from your personal trainer. You read two books about it and even ordered a monthly magazine focused on weight-lifting.

By going to the health club, you began meeting a lot of your health goals. Also, you discovered a whole new group of friends to hang out with who share the love of the sport. You have a new-found interest that brings you a lot of interest, joy, and companionship.

So, many possibilities and wonderful things that you hadn't encountered in life before became available to you because you pursued something of interest.

Your bliss doesn't have to be only one thing, but it can be a collection of things you love to do.

Put these strategies to work to follow your bliss and enjoy the wonders your life will offer:

1. Make a Bliss List. List 5 things that make you happy. Do it quickly without worrying about what you'll choose.

   *Perhaps your list will look something like this: spending time with my children, reading, meeting my financial goals, learning new things, and working with numbers.

✳ Your Bliss List determines what paths you might want to follow in life.

2. Circle the items you have yet to pursue. Put your focus on the items on your Bliss List that you want to go after now.

3. Schedule some time to follow your bliss. If you're spending too much time doing things that lack an interest or happiness factor for you, you're wasting precious moments. When will you go after your circled Bliss items? Mark it in your calendar now.

4. Acknowledge apprehension and then proceed ahead. It's normal to feel a certain amount of fear of the unknown whenever you're about to introduce changes into your life.

   ✳ Tell yourself that if it's really what you want to do, you deserve to follow your bliss, even if it means having to face your fears.

5. Open the doors. After you're involved in doing what brings you joy, you'll learn more and notice the opportunities related to your pursuit.

   ✳ Take advantage of the chances to excel related to the sources of your joyful pastime.

6. Revel in your new-found happiness. It's exciting to begin your own adventure doing something you've wanted to do for quite some time.

    * Allow yourself to fully experience the positive emotions that come from following through with your desires. You deserve it!

You can only imagine the wonders and riches that await you when you pursue the job, living situation, relationship, hobby, or education that will make you happy. Start following your bliss.

3. "Life Is Without Meaning. You Bring The Meaning To It. The Meaning Of Life Is Whatever You Ascribe It To Be. Being Alive Is The Meaning."

You might be seeking the meaning of your life or even asking yourself, "Why am I here?" or "What is my purpose?" This Joseph Campbell quote provides an excellent answer to these questions.

Campbell starts out this quote by stating that the concept of life, in and of itself, lacks a meaning. On its own, life is empty. It is nothing. Then, he goes on further to say that each individual, on their own, contributes the meaning to their own life.

Campbell believed that each of us determines our own meaning by how we live our lives. The very fact that you're alive gives your life meaning, according to Campbell. One theory on the overall lesson in this quote is that only you bring meaning to your own life and you do it simply by living it. No one and nothing else can make your existence meaningful.

Consider these tips to benefit from this Joseph Campbell quote:

1. Give up struggling to figure out why you're here. If you wonder about the purpose for your existence, let go of the incessant questioning.

2. Accept that you're deserving of life. Regardless of what's happened in your past or the mistakes you've made, you deserve to be here, simply because you are here.

3. Make the connection between your desires and your life's purpose. Let what you want in life drive you to "create" your purpose. The fruits of your labor are your purpose.

4. Decide to live a conscious, purposeful life. Stay aware of the time you have on this earth and how you're spending it. When you do these things, you'll be compelled to live an enriched and purposeful life.

Rather than spending time questioning your life, focus on designing, constructing, and carrying out the very existence you yearn for. By doing these things, you give meaning to your own life.

4. "When You Make The Sacrifice In Marriage, You're Sacrificing Not To Each Other But To Unity In A Relationship."

Joseph Campbell's quotes on relationships are powerful and filled with knowledge about enriching your emotional connections. This particular quotation focuses on the importance of sacrifice in love relationships. To sacrifice is to give up something that you want.

Campbell's quote indicates sacrifice is sometimes necessary to sustain the peace and closeness in your marriage.

Your self-deprival is more than an appeasement of your spouse. It is strengthening the foundation of your relationship. It is for the benefit of the "whole," your unity.

To gain clarity of this quote, think about a recent time when you wanted to do something different than what your partner wanted.

Maybe you made plans to spend a Saturday with your friends, but your spouse felt you should spend the afternoon with him (or her) instead. You argued that you hadn't seen your friends in over two months and that the two of you are together most evenings during the week anyway.

Campbell's quote would lead us to believe that if you would have spent the morning with your friends and then sacrificed your afternoon with them to be with your spouse, it would be wise to view that sacrifice as protecting the sanctity of your relationship rather than giving in to your spouse's demands.

If you can view your future sacrifices in your marriage in this way, you'll feel surer about making those sacrifices, knowing that you're preserving the closeness in and emotional quality of your marriage as a whole.

Put these strategies to work in your marriage to enhance that unity:

1. Examine your argumentative and disagreeable behaviors. Do you do everything you can to avoid arguments and unsavory disagreements? If not, explore within yourself the reasons for these unhelpful actions.

   *Admit to yourself what you see as the error of your own ways.

   * Change your behavior if you believe it will be helpful.

2. Know your priorities and live your life according to them. What are the top 5 most important things or people in your life? Those are your priorities.

   ✳When you establish your priorities, it makes sense to live your life according to them.

   ✳ Making decisions is less painful and much easier when you take your priorities into account.

3. Listen. Your spouse is bound to tell you what they want and need from you. How often do they do that and do you listen? When they tell you their needs, are you paying close attention and working with them to ensure both your lives are happy?

4. Preserve the sanctity of your marriage through your everyday actions. When you keep the importance of your relationship in mind each day, you'll enjoy the benefits of a coveted, well-cared-for union with your spouse.

If your marriage is one of your priorities, then the sacrifices you make for it are worth whatever you gave up to strengthen the connection in your relationship.

5. "The Big Question Is Whether You Are Going To Be Able To Say A Hearty Yes To Your Adventure."

Do you follow the same routine, day after day? You get up in the morning, go to work, come home, take out the garbage, and go to bed. On the weekends, you see a few friends or spend time with family members. If so, you might feel like something is missing.

This Joseph Campbell quote charges us to view our lives as an incredible journey. He seems to want us to put our all into living our lives and even refers to life as an "adventure." The quote implies that we don't have to make our lives interesting, fun, and enriching, but that we are asked to—it's "the big question," according to Campbell.

Furthermore, his use of the word, "hearty," makes an interesting impact in the quote because Campbell's implication is that you have a choice to fully embrace and take a full-spirited involvement with life and to do everything possible to live your life to the fullest extent.

In a sense, this quote challenges you to go whole-hog into life and turn it into the biggest adventure you'll ever know.

Use these methods to help you live your life to the fullest:

1. Recognize that you have choices about your life. Each day, you agree to live where you live, do the work you do, and have the types of relationships you have. You're choosing even though you think you're not.

   * Do you want to change your life and live your "adventure?"

   * Are you already living your adventure?

2. Delve into any reasons holding you back from saying, "yes" to your "adventure." Are you afraid to go after what you want? Do you feel you're not worthy of living the life you want? Do you think your personal history is holding your back?

3. Ask for support from close friends and family. If there are things you wish to do but are unsure how to go about them, let your partner and others close to you know that you yearn to do something and need support and ideas regarding how to do it.

4. Just go for it. You've likely been in situations in the past, whether they were at work, playing sports, or in relationships, when you wanted something badly enough that you just "went for it."

✳You can adapt this same determined attitude and create the life you want.

Focusing your efforts to chase after the life you desire can provide you with many rewarding experiences. Keep your head in the "game" of your life by remaining focused on living your most fantastic adventure ever.

6. "It Is By Going Down Into The Abyss That We Recover The Treasures Of Life. Where You Stumble, There Lies Your Treasure."

Joseph Campbell addressed many topics in his writings, speeches, and interviews. One subject he concentrated on was dealing with difficult challenges in life. This particular quote refers to a challenge as an "abyss." This metaphor is perfect because your emotions really can drop you into a deep dark place, like an abyss, whenever you're facing a major life difficulty.

Campbell shares in this quote that he believes that the most salient, important gifts we get from life come out of the experience of a tough life trauma. According to Campbell, we somehow gain much more than we lose during a tragedy.

Campbell thought that tragedy and triumph are deeply connected and that, in essence, you'll "recover" something beautiful and special from a challenge. If you're having a rough time, you'll also discover a "treasure."

Incorporate these methods into your life to emerge triumphantly from difficult situations:

1. Accept that you'll have tough times. The nature in life is that situations will occur that bring heartache and pain.

2. Allow yourself to feel the pain. As difficult as it may be, letting yourself think and feel whatever your thoughts and feelings are during a life crisis is necessary, and even useful.

3. Recognize your "treasures." Maybe you met and made a new friend at the hospital where your parent is dealing with serious illness or you learned something of value for the future from going through a personal tragedy and related suffering.

    ✳ Try to remind yourself that, "Maybe something positive will come out of this."

4. Maintain hope. Faith and hope can get you through a lot of trials and tribulations. Even if you sometimes expect the worst, you can still hope for the best.

During life's toughest times, Joseph Campbell believes you can discover some of life's most precious gifts. Recognize that the paradox of tragedy is that it is often accompanied by triumph.

7. "Opportunities To Find Deeper Powers Within Ourselves Come When Life Seems Most Challenging."

One of the difficulties you'll likely contend with from time to time is feeling like you have no control in certain situations. Yet, this quotation from Joseph Campbell brings the elements of power into a whole new perspective.

In this quote, Campbell says that you'll have chances to discover the power inside you at the times in life when you're being challenged. He believed that the most difficult situations provide you with options to find your own enriched personal power.

This explanation seems to negate itself because we tend to think of challenges as taking away options rather than increasing them. However, Campbell reminds us that other opportunities exist that we can profit from in new ways during those challenging times.

Had we not experienced a challenge, we would not have seen the new options that challenge provided.

He seems to be reminding us to find the power to look for something deeper, something better, and something beyond the challenge itself. And during that act, we develop and wield a new power over our lives.

Apply these tips to live a richer life after experiencing a challenge:

1. Resolve to find your personal power. During a life crisis, it can be difficult to find your way. But if you remind yourself that you'll discover something to help you get through it, you are, in a sense, creating that power. When you take the bull by the horns, you prevail.

2. Recognize there are many ways to emerge from a crisis. Regardless of how you make your way through, know that you can be stronger and better than ever.

Although no one wants to go through a challenge, you can come out on the other side with a sense of strength and a promise to yourself to live your best life from that moment forward.

8. "What Each Must Seek In His Life Never Was On Land Or Sea. It Is Something Out Of His Own Unique Potentiality For Experience, Something That Never Has Been And Never Could Have Been Experienced By Anyone Else."

You may be living your life with the idea in mind that you're looking for something and trying to seek out the "key" or purpose of your life. In this Joseph Campbell quote, he makes it clear that there's no physical place on earth where you'll find your "answer."

Campbell reminds us that each of our life experiences is completely unique and that even though there's potential there, we must each find our own way. Each of us is different and unique, just like a snowflake.

Although there have been millions born before us and millions will be born after us, it's up to each individual to discover their own sense of self and live their own life.

To increase your self-understanding and go after the life you deserve, put these suggestions into action:

1. Acknowledge that you're unique. No one else is exactly like you. You're it. No one can live the life that you can. Then, relish in this idea for a bit. You're pretty special.

2. Realize a physical location doesn't hold any power. Regardless of where you live, you can express your unique sense of self and tap into your potential there.

3. Know that even if you model after others, your experience is still your own. Although you may follow in the footsteps of someone you respect, what you experience belongs only to you.

Your uniqueness ensures that your purpose and life depends singularly on you and what you do with the days you have here on earth. You're an original and that's a wonderful thing to know.

9. "We Must Let Go Of The Life We Have Planned, So As To Accept The One That Is Waiting For Us."

Clearly one of the most profound quotations by Joseph Campbell, this saying reminds us that our life doesn't always go the way we hoped for or expected it to. Tragedies and detours occur.

Maybe you lost someone you could barely fathom losing. Or perhaps you thought you'd eventually complete college, but something always stopped you.

Campbell advises that while you're focusing on the life you had hoped for, your life, here and now, is passing you by. Campbell's suggestion is to simply accept what's in front of you right now and put your heart and soul into the life that's waiting for you. This may mean leaving the past behind.

For example, maybe you experienced a great tragedy by losing a child or spouse. Have you stayed in the pain of those losses and spent many precious moments wondering "what if" that person would have lived and wishing they had?

Yet when you look around you, you have a life full of close friends and people who love you and maybe even other children that might feel a bit slighted by what they feel is the loss of your focus and attention over these recent years. They may be waiting for you and needing you now.

Your current life is, in essence, living and breathing all around you. Avoid letting yourself live in the past when your present life is right there waiting for you.

Follow through with these suggestions today to live the life that's waiting for you:

1. Complete a self-inventory of your overall thoughts about your life. Sit down and go through what you truly think about your life and how you really feel about it. Do you wish things would have gone differently? Do you live with the weight of old regrets?

   *Get in touch with how you feel about your existence.

2. Let go. Release old, unnecessary negativity and feelings. Something in your past might have gone wrong. You might have made mistakes that brought unimaginably painful consequences to you at the time.

* Make the decision to put away the unhelpful thoughts and feelings for good.

* Write them all in a list and then tear it up, burn it, or even bury the list if you prefer.

* Tell yourself, "This is it. I'm done hurting about these things."

3. Start anew. What if you were to really plug in to the life you have right now? Adopt an inspiring mantra. For example, "I have this life and I'm going to live it to the fullest in every way I can." Go forth with renewed interest, plans, and gusto. Give this life your best effort!

If you believe you've put your life on hold for a lot of different reasons that you're unable to change, re-commit to yourself and your current existence. Some great things will happen.

Summary

We can learn from the wisdom and knowledge of the sages that have shared their messages with the world. Joseph Campbell is one such teacher. Each of these quotes provides a valuable life lesson that you can benefit from.

For your best results, start applying these strategies to your life today.

Yes, it will take some effort. In fact, it might become the most monumental endeavor you've ever set out to accomplish. But it will be filled with treasures and triumphs you can only dream about now.

A fulfilling life is waiting and it's yours for the taking!

ABOUT PATRICK DAHDAL

The founder and creator of NLPQ. International Trainer of NLP.
International Master Trainer of NLPQ. Master Coach. Trained in NLP,
Neuro-Semantics, Energy Psychology, Hypnotherapy, Time Lines and
Quantum Psychology. Researched, studied and taught quantum physics,
biology, neuro-science, eastern philosophies and western psychology.
Developer of several effective and transformative training and coaching
programs such as 'The NLPQ Practitioner, Master Practitioner and Trainer
Certification Programs', 'The Limitless Program', 'Matrix Exploded' plus
more.

Patrick has trained and coached thousands of individuals and businesses
around the world to realizing their full potential and purpose.

For more information about Patrick's trainings and coaching programs
visit us at:

http://www.NLPuniversity.co.uk

http://www.TheLimitlessProgram.com

http://www.LiveImprovementEvents.com

Made in the USA
Coppell, TX
11 November 2020